L'ATELIER

of Alain

DUCASSE

Designers: Rampazzo & Associés

Stylist: Laurence Mouton

Editorial coordinators: Didier Elena, Elisa Vergne

Text copyright © Jean-François Revel for the text of L'Atelier

English translation by Isabel Varea / Ros Schwartz Translations, London

© 1998, HACHETTE LIVRE (Hachette Pratique, French edition)

© 2000, HACHETTE LIVRE (Hachette Pratique, English edition)

Distributed exclusively throughout the World, excluding France, by John Wiley & Sons, Inc.

John Wiley & Sons, Inc.

605 Third Avenue

New York, NY 10158-0012

United States of America

Phone 212.850.6000

FAX 212.850.6088

www.wiley.com

2 4 6 8 10 9 7 5 3 1

Printed in Italy

Library of Congress Card Number: (Available upon Request)

ISBN 0-471-37673-6

L'ATELIER
of Alain
DUCASSE

THE ARTISTRY OF A MASTER CHEF AND HIS PROTÉGÉS

FOREWORD BY PATRICIA WELLS

INTRODUCTION BY JEAN-FRANÇOIS REVEL
OF THE ACADÉMIE FRANÇAISE

TEXT BY BÉNÉDICT BEAUGÉ

PHOTOGRAPHS BY HERVÉ AMIARD

Under the direction of Philippe Lamboley

WILEY

JOHN WILEY & SONS, INC.

New York • Chichester • Weinheim • Brisbane • Singapore • Toronto

CON

T E N T S

Alain Ducasse is a man obsessed: obsessed with perfection, sharing, aesthetics, taste, *savoir-faire,* and much more. Unquestionably the most dynamic chef working in France today, he has a decidedly modern and open-minded vision of his art. He is delighted by the turn of events over the last half-century: "Today, cookery is no longer a secret world. Fifty years ago, it took a chef several decades to learn his trade, because his masters jealously guarded their recipes and techniques, and would only share them in their own good time."

But another problem has arisen in recent years. Although young chefs can progress rapidly by learning from books or working under the tutelage of other chefs, they do not necessarily know where to go to exercise their talents. All the top jobs are taken and openings for senior staff in the kitchens of France's temples of gastronomy are rare. Alain Ducasse's advice to young cooks is to head for the provinces. There, they can celebrate the fruit, vegetables, fish, seafood, meat and poultry of each region. They can meet and work with local producers, stockbreeders, fishermen and wine growers. His dream is to see battalions of young chefs trained in his atelier conquering the four corners of France.

Convinced that French cuisine is too solemn, too academic and too tedious, Alain Ducasse tries to make his art more accessible and creative. In his view, skillfully arranged ingredients on a plate are not enough to satisfy the customer!

In his own kitchen, he puts his principles of quality and originality into practice. None of his recipes relies entirely on French culinary traditions, but neither are the glories of the past consigned to oblivion. He transforms *pithiviers* – a classic Loire Valley dish usually consisting of puff pastry filled with almond cream – into a flavorsome Provençal vegetable pie. He enlivens an impeccably fresh and simply cooked turbot with oysters, mussels, clams and razor clams, enhanced by a hint of butter, a little *crème fraîche* and white wine.

Ducasse's cuisine is refined without being precious, and each of his wonderfully fragrant dishes is a work of art in itself.

Patricia Wells
Paris, 27 July 1998

L'Atelier

The Ducasse Paradox

As there are legendary actors of the past and great orators whose voices have been silent for centuries, so there are giants in the history of cookery. How did Molière, Talma, Champmeslé or Adrienne Lecouvreur act, move and speak on stage? How did Cicero and Bossuet articulate, gesticulate and inflect their speech to underscore their glorious command of language? What flavor, consistency or aroma greeted seventeenth-century gourmets as they tasted François La Varenne's bisque (which bore no resemblance to what we call bisque today)? What did eighteenth-century gastronomes experience as they raised to their lips the oyster and truffle sauce created by Marin, author of *Les Dons de Comus*? How did it feel to savor for the first time Antonin Carême's *darnes de saumon et galantines d'anguilles au beurre de Montpellier, bordure de ravigote vert tendre* (salmon steaks and eel galantine with Montpellier butter[1] with pale green ravigote), created for the wedding feast of Prince Jérôme Bonaparte and Catherine of Württemberg? We can, of course, read the accounts of the

creators themselves and the testimony of those of their contemporaries fortunate enough to sit at tables spread with the results of their artistry. But a musical score does not exist in its own right, or, at least, it has no more than a virtual existence. Its interpretation depends entirely upon the performer. In *La Riviera d'Alain Ducasse* (Albin Michel, 1992), I read the recipe for that Monegasque culinary curiosity redolent of the Mediterranean, "*Barbajuans*", a kind of ravioli, stuffed with herbs, or with seasonal red squash or leeks, served as a starter. Just reading about them made my mouth water. However, when I actually tasted them for the first time, prepared by Ducasse himself, or under his supervision, at the Louis XV in Monaco, the flavors, fragrances and textures far transcended the qualities suggested by my dutiful study of the recipe. What the non-specialist, however well-informed, cannot grasp is the "*je ne sais quoi*", the *savoir-faire*. No doubt we should be equally astounded if we were to travel back in time and sample a Carême dish prepared by Carême, or one of Nignon's creations, prepared by Nignon. But let us turn our eager attention to the tables of those culinary geniuses who, like us, are alive and well, for no text, no reconstruction can compare with attending our own private performance by Molière of works by Molière.

When we taste the cuisine of a very great artist for the first time, our initial thought is: "I had no idea such things were possible." This spontaneous reaction clearly indicates the presence of some indefinable talent. Between reading the recipe on the page and the actual making of the dish by its creator, something wonderful happens. An intrinsic feature of every kind of art is the importance of execution, which goes far beyond mere imagination. Of course, imagination is crucial. It distinguishes the inventor from those excellent cooks who make an invaluable, indispensable, and irreplaceable contribution by passing on traditional skills. But tradition itself would die out without the creativity of those who, every now and again, return to the source and rethink the basic concepts, so reviving, prolonging and rejuvenating the old ways. And creativity would be nothing without tradition.

Alain Ducasse is not one of those chefs who claim to owe nothing to the teachings and tricks of home cooking, to that precious knowledge handed down from generation to generation for hundreds, even thousands, of years. "The gastronomic memory of a region," he says, "is based on recipes concocted in obscurity by gifted cooks, and we don't know from where or from whom they have learned their secrets. In borrowing from them, I am fulfilling a sacred

duty: I am rescuing hidden gastronomic treasures from oblivion." His creative culinary style never loses touch with the traditional ways of countryside and coast. Their legacy, he says, serves as "a kind of reference point." Too many chefs proudly imagine that they can create something out of nothing and end up creating nothing at all. Even some great cooks have been led astray by this ancient illusion. Among them was that mysterious but undeniably talented seventeenth-century artist known only by the initials, L.S.R. In his *Art de bien traiter* (1674), he scathingly condemns the fashionable recipe for broiled mackerel, calling it "a delusion of the petite-bourgeoisie and ignorant plebeians". According to L.S.R., these poor misguided people arrange the mackerel on a bed of fennel, while he himself places them straight onto the gridiron, to which they will not stick, provided they are very fresh. Good for him!

Between reading the recipe on the page and the actual preparation of the dish by its creator, something wonderful happens.

ALAIN DUCASSE is a man of strong personality, conscious of his own worth, but this does not mean that he fails to recognize his indebtedness, not only to ancient tradition but also to the modern masters who have helped to train him and enable him to discover his own style: Michel Guérard, Gaston Lenôtre, Roger Vergé and, above all, the sensitive, meditative Alain Chapel, the philosopher-cook of Mionnay. Many artists refuse to acknowledge the talents of their elders or rivals. That same L.S.R. congratulates himself in the foreword to his book. "I was right," he declares, "to reform that out-dated and disgusting manner of preparing and serving food." Certainly, from the mid-seventeenth century onwards, French cuisine underwent a continuous process of renewal. The innovative chef, the driving force behind these changes, achieved celebrity status. "He is pampered, humored and, when angry, placated", wrote Sébastien Mercier in *Tableau de Paris* (1786). This period saw the resurgence of the megalomaniac cook, that symbol of civilization who first appeared on the scene under the Roman Empire, Antiquity's culinary golden age. Even the mighty Carême, in his *Art de la cuisine française au dix-neuvième siècle* (1833), maintained that *haute cuisine* barely existed before him and would decline after him. If we are to believe him, he owed nothing to anyone in the past and no future cook would ever be his equal! He did, however, make an exception of one of the most imaginative of his eighteenth-century precursors: Vincent La Chapelle, author of *Cuisinier moderne* (1733). The overwhelming desire to be seen as the only genius of his time, indeed of all time, is not confined to masters

of the gastronomic art. Even so, it has been exacerbated by the current trend for turning chefs into media stars. But the whole notion rests on an historical error: when any art form flourishes, be it cookery, painting or music, it is because there is an abundance of talent. Competition stimulates invention and the overall standard of artistic achievement rises. Alain Ducasse is well aware of this.

He is even more aware that great cuisine relies first and foremost on the authenticity, quality and freshness of the ingredients. On 23 January 1998, Alain Ducasse invited me to lunch at his Paris restaurant in the Hôtel Le Parc. Halfway through the meal in the little private dining room in the center of his kitchens, from where he oversees the various sections of his brigade, he served me a Breton turbot with asparagus and crawfish, topped with a champagne *sabayon*. (We are not talking here about the frothy dessert that Italians call *zabaglione*, but the savory mousseline sauce of the same name). Although a more or less classic dish, it still came as a surprise, due to the split-second precision of the cooking process and, of course, the taste of the *sabayon* ("At present, I'm the one who does it best," confesses Ducasse without false modesty). But most of all it was due to the intrinsic virtue of a turbot fished from the ocean just hours earlier which had not needed to be packed in ice. Hence Ducasse's genuine modesty when he insists that the excellence of the product takes precedence over that of the chef. With his customary verbal dexterity, he seasoned the fish with the aphorism: "Turbot without genius is better than genius without turbot."

In both Paris and Monaco, much of his time and conversation is taken up with the search for ingredients. Cookery extends and ennobles the works of nature. It both relies on and refines nature. Culinary creation depends on good working relationships with scrupulous vegetable growers, honest fishermen whose fish "caught last night" really were landed the night before, and quality livestock breeders. Regions and seasons must be harmonized. John Dory is better in Monaco than in Paris; turbot is better in Paris than in Monaco. Asparagus from the Vaucluse, grown in the alluvial deposits of the Rhône, are, according to Ducasse, tastier and more tender than any other. Suckling lamb is served from February to Easter.

Ducasse has revived the art of the vegetable, relegated for the past 30 years to the rank of accompaniment, with the dispiriting garnish of "baby" vegetables frugally scattered on the plate with the intention of pleasing the eye rather than the palate. He has recreated vegetables as a separate course, using, for example, peas picked the previous day in Nice, which have never seen the inside of a refrigerator or a truck, and which he cooks at the Louis XV with

baby onions, leaves and ribs of lettuce, turnips, carrots, asparagus, baby potatoes and *lardons*. And then, still at the Louis XV in Monaco, he lovingly prepares peas with crushed black truffles, Ligurian olive oil, a little balsamic vinegar and coarse gray salt. Committed to limiting himself to what is available locally, Ducasse does not use the same products in Monaco and Paris. It is less easy to obtain really fresh vegetables in the capital than in the principality. There are no Mediterranean imports, no tomatoes, no olive oil, on his Parisian menu. The accent here is far more on the creamier cuisine of northern France, with *béchamels* and a return to the noble sauces inherited, but not slavishly copied, from the Carêmian repertoire. For, even when making sauces, Ducasse stays close to nature, distancing himself from the methods of Carême. He does not bind the pan juices, but serves them just as they come from the saucepan, skillet or stew pot. He has no time for d*emi-glace* or *grande espagnole,* which were reworked by Édouard Nignon at the beginning of the twentieth century. Nor will you find on his stoves any sauce which has not been wholly and directly made with fresh products purchased by Ducasse himself, without recourse to industrially manufactured essences or concentrates, not even the best ones. During that same lunch, he confided sardonically: "The vast majority of sauce bases are supplied by a multinational food manufacturer, even to restaurants with the most stars!" "Which ones? Which ones?" I cried. But, with a dismissive wave of the hand, my host kept his secret.

Even before the era of non-organic farming, before grazing animals were force-fed on meat-reinforced meal or poultry fattened on fish meal, chefs and connoisseurs were engaged in a perpetual search for products of the best and most authentic provenance. In *Les Éloges de la cuisine française* (1933), with a foreword by Sacha Guitry, we can read the account by Édouard Nignon, chef of the Larue (Marcel Proust's favorite restaurant), of the monthly meals prepared for a group of food-loving friends. These gourmets met once a month, each time in a different region of France, and each time enjoying a different menu. The idea was to find the best natural, seasonal products of each locality, and have them prepared by

an eminent chef whose artistic skills would exploit and refine their innate qualities. Audiger first introduced peas to the French court in 1660, starting a craze which even earned the royal seal of approval. His book *La maison réglée* (1697) offers a wealth of advice on how they should be picked and cooked, without altering the flavor. At the same time, Louis XIV set up his own kitchen garden at Versailles under La Quintinie's supervision. Even in Antiquity, when there was no industrial pollution or artificial overproduction to contaminate or dull the flavor of fresh produce, it is remarkable what extraordinary attention was paid to place and provenance by the gastronomic writers of the day. They offered as much detailed advice on the place where a particular animal should be hunted or a certain type of fish caught, or the region where a certain variety of vegetable should be grown or type of fruit harvested, as they did on methods of preparation, cooking and seasoning. According to Archestratus (4th century BCE), the only good sturgeon came from Rhodes. The only decent mullet was that

fished in the lake flowing into the sea between Priene and Miletus in Asia Minor, far superior to that caught out at sea. Only baby eels from Athens, and large eels from the Strait of Messina – preferably caught at Reggio – were acceptable. The heightened sensibility of the ancient epicures sometimes achieved astounding levels of precision. In *Satires,* Book II, satire VII, Juvenal writes of a gourmet by the name of Montanus, who lived in the second century, and who "from the first mouthful could distinguish an oyster from Circie (on the southwest coast of Italy), from one taken from the rocks of Lake Lucrino or the waters of Rutupiae (which became Richborough, in the English county of Kent), and, at first glance, could guess from which shore a sea urchin had been picked". The same might be said of some olive oil connoisseurs, who can determine whether an oil originates from Tuscany or Liguria, Provence or Andalucia.

NEVERTHELESS, unlike any of his predecessors, Ducasse has something new to say about the novel situation with which he is confronted. And he is not merely repeating what every intelligent cook has always known, that all good cuisine is based on good ingredients. These days it is a grim daily struggle to obtain a regular supply of fresh, authentic products. The French consume five times as many tomatoes as they

> This example shows how a conscientious artist cannot be content to let nature dictate. He must revive it.

did twenty years ago. But can they really be called tomatoes? A tomato grown on a plant genuinely rooted in the soil and ripened only by the sun's rays, is more difficult to find than caviar. The soggy, tasteless, flaccid, red flesh of the inferior fruits currently produced is not even worth the water it takes to spray them. Of course, Ducasse does manage to find real Provençal tomatoes, and even instigates their cultivation. On the hills of Valbonne he has succeeded in persuading growers to produce the original yellow tomato, just as the conquistadors discovered it in Peru in the sixteenth century. This example shows how a conscientious artist cannot be content to let nature dictate. He must revive it. No

longer is it the good product that makes for good cuisine; it is good cuisine that enables the good product to reappear, for it opens up a market of knowledgeable and appreciative consumers. This is what happens when, in his Paris restaurant, Ducasse serves his "*lard paysan*", breast of farm-reared pork, salted, rubbed with black pepper and dried in old, lightly ventilated sheds, then desalted for 36 hours before cooking. Imagine the degree of commitment on the part of the farmers who devote time, patience and money to rearing the 450-lb animal from which this morsel is cut, and the unsparing effort put into the preparation of the meat. In these modern times, the land is far removed from nature, and nature has found refuge in *haute cuisine*. For now nature has become too expensive; in the kitchen, as elsewhere, it has become a supreme luxury.

BUT COOKERY is not only about grafting invention onto nature, it is also about technique, equipment, organization and management. As far as equipment is concerned, Ducasse uses copper saucepans made to his specification, whose bases and sides are 1 ¼ inches rather than 1 inch thick. He has invented a rotisserie, with an "Alain Ducasse spit"; redesigned carving, slicing and chopping knives, and devised a mortar in Breton granite, solid oak and brushed stainless steel. When it comes to kneading, pounding, crushing, mixing and beating, while still preserving and enhancing tastes and aromas, there is no substitute for this ancestral tool, which has disappeared from most pantries. Ducasse now heads a small enterprise manufacturing state-of-the-art kitchen equipment and furniture, such as chopping blocks, storage units, ovens and cookware.

Every gastronomic revolution is partly the result of the development of new kitchen equipment. A striking example is the invention in the seventeenth century, of a large cooking range known as a "*potager*". Previously, food was cooked in the hearth, either in a pot suspended over the fire, or on a spit, making it difficult to control temperatures. The *potager* had between twelve and twenty burners, allowing temperatures to be far more finely regulated. It was now possible to cook over a slow or fast heat, to bake in the oven, simmer, broil, fry or braise food, or keep it warm over a gentle heat. The master chef could use all and any of these methods on the same range as and when he wished. He could also prepare the refinements required for the various courses of the meal: *coulis*, *salpicons*, purées, *mirepoix, blonds de veau*, glazes and *demi-glaces*, all of which first appeared on the French culinary scene in the eighteenth century.

Antonin Carême was among the first to realize the need for a radical reorganization of the whole system of food preparation. He sought to rationalize the work of the brigade, as L.S.R. had done 150 years earlier, outlining in his *Art de bien traiter*, a strategy requiring the combined talents of a military commander and a sophisticated interior designer. Alain Ducasse has to fulfill even more roles than his venerable forebears. He is simultaneously head chef, company president, team leader, college principal and director of public relations. He is also a great communicator, personnel manager, talent-spotter and teacher.

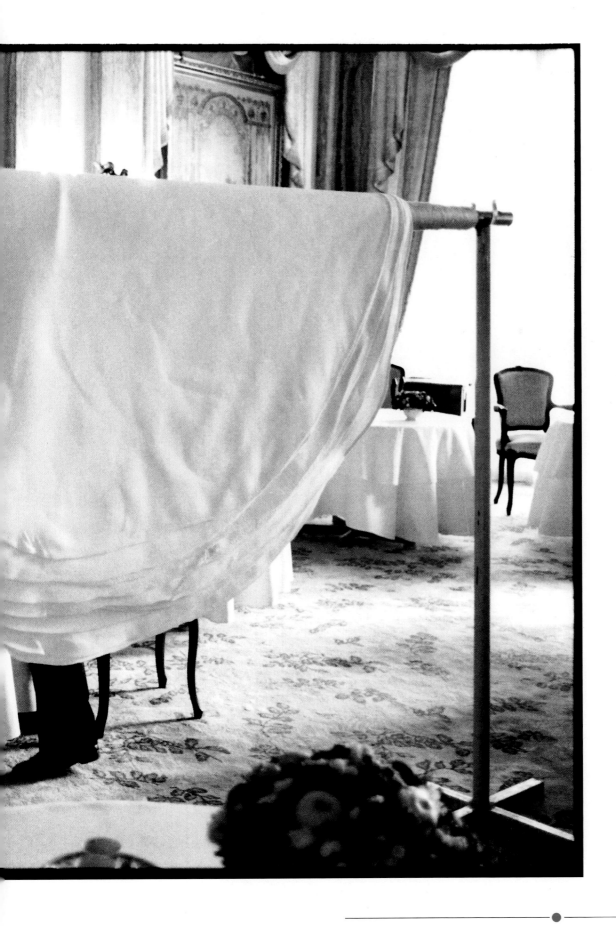

AT THE AGE of just 42 and in only 12 years as the man with ultimate responsibility, he has employed more than 500 people. Had he not been a good manager, how could he have survived in a situation like that at his Paris restaurant? How could he make a profit from an organization where 53 employees, including 20 kitchen staff, work together to please a maximum of 50 customers? And Ducasse has no qualms about adding unashamedly and even slightly provocatively: "I'm the most expensive restaurant in the world". He says it, not so much out of vanity, but simply to stress his ability to attract enough gastronomes willing to pay the same price as a music lover would pay for a seat in the stalls at la Scala Milan.

Ultimately, though, what makes Ducasse unique is what I would call the "Ducasse paradox". He is the first chef-restaurateur who has dared to admit openly, and even elevate to the status of a doctrine, his belief that a chef can serve his customers with the world's finest food without constantly slaving at the stove himself. Of course, we have long become used to the absences of some of the biggest names in French cuisine, who are more likely to be found in Japan, Hong Kong or the United States than in their kitchens in Lyon or Paris. But it used to be a sort of shameful secret. Diners wishing to compliment the chef would be told that he was on the phone or had just slipped out for a moment – even if he was actually in Singapore.

DUCASSE BROKE THE TABOO in 1996, when he took over the great Joël Robuchon's restaurant in Paris – a risky endeavor if ever there was one – while keeping on his own establishment in Monaco. He had three stars in Monaco. Robuchon had three stars in Paris. How would the 1997 *Guide Michelin* react? Take away the six stars then wait and see? Even in the jet age, could the same chef prepare the finest imaginable cuisine in two kitchens over 600 miles apart, without cheating? "You cannot be a genius in two places at once" retorted Gilles Pudlowski, witty restaurant critic of *Le Point*. In 1997, *Michelin* opted for an interim solution: it retained three stars in Paris, while removing one in Monaco. But the fundamental question remained unanswered: can a single chef excel in two places simultaneously? The answer came in the 1998 guide, which restored the third star to the Monaco restaurant: yes, it can be done.

Other great artists of gastronomy, such as Pierre Gagnaire of Paris's three-star Balzac, and Olivier Roellinger of the two-star Maison de Bricourt at Cancale, believe that this is an ambiguous and uncertain state of affairs. According to them, customers paying between $150 and $300 (1,000-2,000 *francs*) per head are entitled to expect the chef to be in the kitchen supervising the whole operation himself, as they themselves insist on doing. Nevertheless, in Ducasse's case, experience told: between 1996 and 1998, the quality at the Louis XV did not deteriorate while, at the avenue Raymond-Poincaré, the highest standards were set, in a style quite different from Robuchon's. "When my colleagues saw that I was coping perfectly well in Paris they stopped calling me," Ducasse confided with a hint of irony. "They no longer felt the need to check up on me."

So the gamble paid off. Some occasionally quote a single precedent. In the 1930s, the "Mère Brazier" had two sets of three stars: one for the restaurant in Lyon and one for the second restaurant at Col de la Luère, outside the city. But there is no comparison. The Mère Brazier's two neighboring establishments offered the same cuisine, but the downtown restaurant was open in winter and the Col de la Luère one in summer. In fact, the one and only restaurateur shuttled between the two according to the time of year.

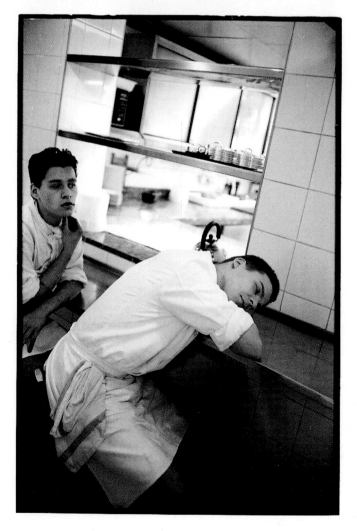

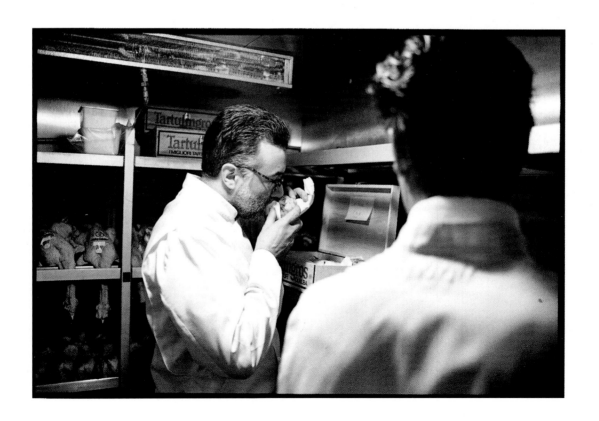

Ducasse, meanwhile, works to a revolutionary principle: "I have a very modern way of thinking; the chef is there to lead the team and not just to sit behind the piano." When we see the encyclopedic menus served by Antonin Carême to hundreds of diners, do we honestly believe that he prepared everything himself? Nevertheless everything was perfect, and all Carême's own work. According to Ducasse, the chef writes the score, which "can be interpreted in the best way possible by a perfectly trained brigade".[2] Franck Cerutti in Monte Carlo and Jean-François Piège in Paris are Ducasse's right-hand men, who do much more than simply put his ideas into practice. Between all three there is a constant creative exchange of ideas. Several other artists contribute to the recipes devised in L'Atelier, for it is the concept of the "atelier" that matters most to Ducasse, as it did to renaissance painters. He also realizes that his present protégés will soon become independent, like so many of his former associates who now run their own, highly prestigious restaurants, not only in France but also in Italy, the United States, Great Britain and Japan.

The prospect of introducing *haute gastronomie* to a much wider market naturally raises economic objections, for, as Ducasse constantly stresses, it is a very expensive business. But his atelier concept does allow us to envisage mass reproduction of the art of the great chefs, creating a relationship comparable to that existing in the fashion industry between ready-to-wear and *haute couture*.

When Paul Bocuse heard the news in June 1998 that the contract to cater for the football fans that would pack French stadiums during the World Cup competition had been awarded to an American fast-food firm, he proclaimed the urgent need to "resist the imperialism of the hamburger covered with ketchup and drowned with Coca-Cola". Throwing wild accusations of "imperialism" at others is a frequent reaction of those who see themselves as inferior but do to not want to admit their own shortcomings. And budget catering in France certainly is inferior. It is unacceptable, whereas cheap American catering is not. In terms of quality and price, France no longer has the equivalent of the good Italian *tavola calda*, Spanish *tasca* or Greek *taverna*. Even non-starred but good-quality French restaurants are too expensive for most ordinary workers. I am talking here about the everyday establishments, the café-brasseries where office workers and salesclerks go to eat lunch for the price of one or two meal tickets. The whole thing is scandalous! We can discount the "*bons bistrots*", those addresses that gourmets recommend to one another in a whisper, most of which are as expensive as the classier restaurants. In France, we have the university refectory, the school or company canteen, the café that at midday is transformed into a so-called restaurant where vile concoctions are produced in the so-called kitchen, a dark and disgusting subterranean cubbyhole crammed between the toilets and the telephones. None of these could ever rival their American counterparts, which, while not serving real cuisine, do provide wholesome food. In France, there is a gaping void below the expensive top- and medium-grade restaurants.

So let us be grateful that a master chef like Alain Ducasse both constantly reinvents *haute gastronomie* but also has the entrepreneurial skills to influence mass catering with the admirable results of his art and his atelier. Perhaps the "Ducasse paradox" will also be the paradox of the 21st century.

JEAN-FRANÇOIS REVEL
ACADÉMIE FRANÇAISE

---

[1] The recipe for Carême's *beurre de Montpellier* occupies no less than a page! You will find it quoted in chapter 9 of my *Festin en paroles* (latest revised and enlarged edition, Plon, 1995).

[2] See article by Alain Ducasse in *Le Monde*, 25 December 1997.

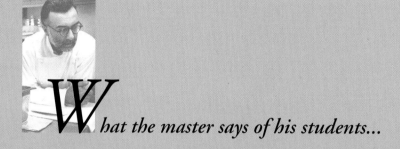

*W*hat the master says of his students...

Franck Cerutti *is the very embodiment of the Mediterranean spirit. It runs in his blood and he expresses it on a daily basis. But he is also a genuine interpreter, an organizer, he doesn't merely do his job. That is why he is the perfect assistant.*

A modest man who always wants to do better, ***Jean-Louis Nomicos*** *can tackle anything in the kitchen; he has done every conceivable job at the Hôtel de Paris. He has now found his own distinctive style and is completely at home as a chef.*

Jean-François Piège *is the epitome of perfectionism: disciplined, professional and loyal. No one can ever achieve the standards he sets. A born leader, always eager to improve the quality of his team.*

Although he is an exceptional sauce chef, ***Sylvain Portay*** *is also the perfect all-rounder: highly organized, he can turn his hand to anything, but always with a "good buddy" kind of attitude. He has given a great deal to his teams.*

Alessandro Stratta *is an indefatigable workhorse. The first to arrive and the last to leave, he has an incredible capacity for work, he is eager to learn and insatiably curious. Hence, his successful career.*

● THE TASTE OF SOIL

Although he was born in Nice, Franck Cerutti spent most of his childhood and teenage years in the mountains behind the city. He found rural life so appealing that, for a time, he thought of becoming a farmer. His family was hardly enthusiastic at the prospect. He then turned his thoughts to being a chef or a sommelier, so as to maintain contact with the products he so loved, and enrolled at hotel school. He began his career in grand hotels, working at Évian and Eden Roc, but quickly became bored. Soon after Jacques Maximin returned to take charge of the Chantecler at the Hotel Negresco, Cerutti wrote to him and was granted an interview. He was hired immediately. This was still a luxury grand hotel, but one that offered his kind of cuisine. He stayed three years.

FRANCK CERUTTI ● *Le Louis XV*

● A LOYAL COLLEAGUE

Then began the Ducasse period. The association was punctuated by occasional breaks, but was nonetheless continuous. Franck Cerutti played a role in all the chef's new endeavors, including his débuts at La Terrasse of the Hôtel Juana and the Hôtel de Paris. Between each spell he went back to work with Maximin, with whom he was to remain for a further two years before moving to Florence's Enoteca Pinchiori, where he hoped to rediscover his Mediterranean roots. Cerutti's most significant career move was the opening of his own restaurant in his home city, two steps away from the market in cours Saleya, the very heart of his world, where he was able to revive a culinary style very similar to that of his great-grandmother. Nevertheless, when Alain Ducasse summoned him for the launch of his Paris restaurant, Cerutti left rue des Ponchettes to supervise the kitchens of the Louis XV.

Jean-louis Nomicos ● *La Grande Cascade*

● CRUCIAL DISCOVERIES

Armed with his diploma, he joined Alain Ducasse's brigade at Juan-les-Pins. At the Hôtel Juan's Terrasse restaurant, he discovered what he describes as "true cuisine", where flavors were concentrated instead of diluted, where the closest possible attention was paid to culinary technique, and only the very finest ingredients were acceptable.

Nomicos began as a *commis* – or trainee – chef , but when a *chef de partie* (head of section) left, he immediately took over the job, and it was in this capacity that he followed Ducasse to the Louis XV. They were to work together for eight years in all, at La Terrasse, the Louis XV but also at the Grill of the Hôtel de Paris (where his boss was Bruno Caironi). The association gave him the chance to travel the world and encounter other cultures. Under Alain Ducasse's tutelage, he discovered new products and whole new worlds of flavors. Jean-Louis Nomicos regards his overseas travels as probably his most valuable asset. After three years as executive chef at La Grande Cascade, a place he loves for the freedom he has found there and the enormously varied clientele, he realizes how hard it is to create his own cuisine day after day, now that his mentor is no longer there to guide him.

● MEMORIES OF SUNDAY LUNCHES

Jean-Louis Nomicos is a child of the south. He was born and spent his childhood in a little village near Aubagne, not far from Marseilles. No one in his immediate family worked in the catering business, but his mother, and especially his grandmother, were excellent cooks and he still has vivid memories of Sunday lunches at his grandparents' house. Perhaps this was why he decided to serve an apprenticeship at Marseilles's Oursinade restaurant, where he learned a very classic style of cuisine, enabling him to achieve his Certificat d'Aptitude Professionnelle, the formal professional qualification.

● PERFUMES AND FLAVORS

A native of Valence, the gateway to Provence, Jean-François Piège wanted to be a gardener. As a child, he was fascinated by the fragrances he discovered when he went to market with his grandmother. It was this love of fresh produce that led him to become a cook. He started in the business in the traditional way, beginning his career at a provincial restaurant, Le Chabichou. Following this, he entered the world of Alain Ducasse for the first time, when he worked under Bruno Cirino's supervision at Château Eza. There he learned the true meaning of the word "demanding". For the first time his superiors inculcated in him a taste for the finest ingredients, a lesson that would be reinforced later when he worked alongside Alain

JEAN-FRANÇOIS PIÈGE ● *Le restaurant Alain Ducasse*

Ducasse. Meanwhile, on Cirino's advice, he applied for a post at the Crillon. He was deeply impressed with Christian Constant's management style: running the kitchen of a hotel of this class is no easy task!

● CONTINUOUS RENEWAL

After completing his military service in the kitchens of the Élysée Palace where he learned classic *grande cuisine*, he was reunited with Bruno Cirino, then presiding over the Élysées du Vernet, before fulfilling his dream of rejoining the Louis XV brigade in Monte Carlo. He took advantage of his three years

there to perfect his skills as a pastry chef and so was raring to go when the Paris restaurant opened. Jean-François Piège enjoys this extremely close collaboration with Alain Ducasse because it teaches him more than merely recipes, it has instilled in him a state of mind. It has taught him to be demanding: to demand only the finest ingredients, to demand that every task be well done, to demand the very best of himself. He has acquired the ability to set himself challenges, and not be content with winning formulae, but each time to find the culinary style best suited to the location.

SYLVAIN PORTAY ● *Ritz Carlton Hotel*

● BETWEEN TWO CONTINENTS

Born at Évian on the shores of Lake Geneva, Sylvain Portay started work at a very early age. At 15, he was already apprenticed to Jean-Louis Palladin at La Table des Cordeliers in Condom, in the *département* of Gers in southwestern France. When Palladin left for Washington to open the Jean-Louis Restaurant, Portay went with him. It was his first encounter with the United States, but not his last. Since that day, Sylvain Portay has spent his working life commuting between the United States and the Mediterranean. On his return to France, he undertook a succession of placements shared with several Alain Ducasse protégés of his generation: the Chantecler with Maximin, La Terrasse with Ducasse himself, the Enoteca Pinchiori in Florence, then a detour to Jean Delaveyne's Camelia in Bougival. But he always longed to return to the States and, on the advice of Jacques Maximin, he became executive chef at Antoine, Newport Beach, an appointment which elevated him to the peak of his profession.

● A WINNING TEAM

Alain Ducasse had just taken over the kitchens at the Hôtel de Paris once again. He entrusted the hotel's Grill Restaurant to Sylvain Portay, who then went on to spend the obligatory period catering to the gourmets of the Riviera. Impressed by Portay's success, Alain Ducasse made him his closest collaborator, appointing him chef at the Louis XV. They proved a winning team: it was at this time that the restaurant was awarded three stars by the *Michelin Guide*. It might have been because Sylvain Portay missed America, or perhaps he wanted to prove himself in his own right, but in 1992 he returned to the United States, initially to join Le Cirque in New York, where he was executive chef for four years. He then took up his present post at San Francisco's Ritz Carlton Hotel where he works under his own name.

● A FAMILIAR WORLD

Alessandro Strata's back-ground is rather different from that of his fellow students. The son of an Italian father and a French-Canadian mother, he comes from a family of hotel keepers and restaurateurs. His childhood and adolescence were spent in the world of catering, trailing after his parents as they took up various posts around the globe. From an early age he came face to face with different culinary traditions and dif-ferent worlds of taste. By the age of 16, he had decided: he would be a chef in a big restaurant! After a period of training in the Californian hotel where his father was manager, he realized that he needed discipline and knowledge if he was to fulfill his ambitions, and enrolled at the California Culinary Insti-tute in San Francisco. After two

A LESSANDRO STRATTA ● *Renoir, Mirage Hotel*

years under the supervision of one of America's most renowned pastry chefs, he joined the staff of the Beverly Hills Hotel. But the work he was required to do there left him disillusioned and full of doubt. With his father's help he became a trainee with Alain Ducasse.

● THE NEED FOR PERFECTION

Alessandro Stratta started at the Louis XV as an apprentice pastry chef. He spent only two weeks in the job. The chef in charge of the *mise en place* – all the operations carried out in the restaurant prior to serving

the meal – fell ill and Stratta was chosen to replace him. He used this opportunity to the best advantage and found the perpetual demand for perfection stimulating but sometimes exhausting. After doing various jobs in the kitchens of the Louis XV, he re-turned to the United States where he was a sauce chef at Le Cirque for a time. From 1989 to 1998, he was *chef de cuisine* at Mary Elaine's at the Phoenician in Scottsdale, Arizona. The winner of a James Beard culinary award in 1998, Alessandro is currently the executive chef of Renoir at the Mirage Hotel in Las Vegas, Nevada.

Products
and Producers

Products

" I do my shopping in the four corners of France."
One could almost say in the four corners of the Earth.

When asked, all Alain Ducasse's students invariably quote the mantra by which the master defines good cuisine: "60% ingredients, 40% technique". They also proclaim loud and clear that they do not consider themselves creators but artisans, technicians whose task it is to elevate each product to its highest degree of excellence. For Ducasse, everything begins with the product: "It is the intrinsic character of the products that determines the type of recipes for which I use them. Products are the foundation on which I build my recipes. I never do it the other way around." Moreover, he proves it every day. Had he not chosen to be a chef, he would have liked to be a "traveler", one of those nineteenth-century explorers who discovered previously unknown lands. Whenever possible, he sets off around the globe, returning with products that he finds intriguing or appealing. He might discover an astonishing variety of cured pork in a remote corner of Italy, or be excited by a particular type of Norwegian cod or Provençal zucchini. In Monaco a few years ago he admitted: "I spend a lot of time looking for the finest products. I use everything the region has to offer, but I do my shopping in the four corners of France." One could almost say in the four corners of the Earth.

● THE "TAGGIASCA" OLIVE

For Alain Ducasse, olives and citrus fruits are, in a way, the "signature" – an important term in his style of cuisine – of the Mediterranean. He confesses to being crazy about Taggiasca olives pitted and macerated in oil, and can devour them by the spoonful. During his "Mediterranean" period, and even more so during his time on the Riviera, olives became an absolutely essential ingredient. Ducasse regards olive oil as his finest culinary tool, transcending all others and reigning supreme in his kitchen. He uses the milder type as a basic cooking oil, for everything from browning to deep frying. The fruity version serves as a condiment, a superior sort of seasoning: a few glistening drops added to a soup, or as a finishing touch to a *jus*, drizzled over vegetables or as a topping to *fromage frais*. But olives are also used for themselves and their derivatives, such as *tapenade* and various kinds of purées.

Between the products of the Nice region and the Ligurian Riviera, there are both similarities and differences. Olives and olive oil are prime examples. On the Italian side, in response to a much wider and more demanding market, olive cultivation and olive oil production have made considerable progress since the end of World War II. On the French side, following the big freeze of 1956 which destroyed almost all the olive groves, the same industries stagnated and had, until recently, fallen into decline. The "Taggiasca" olive (named after the little town of Taggia, inland from San Remo) is the same as the little "cailletier" olive from Nice. Its color changes from green tinged with pink to a deep, almost black, purple when fully ripe. The olive trees grow in terraced rows along the valleys that penetrate deep inland until they reach altitudes of 2,000 – 2,300 feet, the maximum at which the fruit can flourish. It is the very nature of the landscape that gives the olives their special qualities. The

mountains literally plunge into the sea, so that the fruit benefits both from altitude and the proximity of the Mediterranean. While in most regions the olives all ripen at once so that there is only a single harvest, here the season extends from mid-November until late March, creating a distinction between fruit picked at different times.

At Casa Olearia Taggiasca, a small family business, Marco Bonaldo has taken advantage of this to produce different kinds of extra-virgin olive oils with recognizably different flavors. *Albis*, produced right at the start of the season, is new olive oil. The still slightly green olives lend it a particular fruitiness, but without the sharp, bitter tang of Tuscan olives. In the early spring, very ripe, very black olives are picked at altitude. These produce the very delicate, slightly opalescent oil known as *Opalino*. Throughout the winter, the firm manufactures oils of varying flavors, which are combined to create the oil of the year. This is labeled *Bormano*, after Bormanus, the Roman god who protects the region. The olives are harvested by hand and taken to the mill, where they are graded into five sizes. The biggest and best are placed in brine and later pitted and preserved in oil. The next size down will simply be pickled in brine. The third category is reserved for making oil, while the fourth and fifth are set aside to be made into olive pulp for use in manufacturing condiments. The olives are

immediately crushed in the traditional way with a millstone; no better method has yet been invented. There may be faster ways but they do not create such a refined product (this is largely due to the manner in which the pits and the kernel inside them are crushed together). By contrast, a state-of-the-art method is employed to extract the oil. After being pressed between the nylon fiber disks which have now replaced the matting over which the olive pulp used to be spread, thousands of stainless steel blades are passed across the pulp. They pick up the oil which is then drained into another container. You can experiment by dipping a knife blade into an emulsion of oil and water. Only the oil will adhere to the blade, so separating the two fluids. Despite precautions taken with the old system, the mats were inevitably impregnated with the aftertaste of earlier pressings. The new method allows the production of the purest oil under the most hygienic conditions.

● THE GREEN ASPARAGUS OF VILLELAURE

Alain Ducasse was born in Les Landes, an asparagus-producing region, and he admits his passion for wild asparagus. However, when it comes to serving this vegetable in one of his restaurants, he has no hesitation: he prefers the green asparagus of Villelaure. He likes its tenderness, the strong, grassy fragrance of freshly-picked spears, and the delicate note of bitterness that make it such a truly elegant vegetable. He uses it in many ways, and even sprinkles some dishes with thin shavings of raw asparagus cut on a mandolin. This not only allows him to perform one of his favorite tricks: contrasting raw and cooked ingredients; it also reveals the tartness of wild asparagus, not unlike that of young leeks.

The asparagus is a strange vegetable. Only a few varieties of this perennial plant exist but these can appear in different forms depending on the method of cultivation - white, pink, purple, mauve, Provençal green (the color only reaches halfway up the spear), or American green (green all the way up). The rhizomes are planted in light, loose, fresh, fairly damp soil. For several years, the underground stems, or "crowns", produce edible shoots. As soon as the shoots start to emerge, they are earthed up, with only the tips peeping out of the soil. This is done in order to etiolate them, to deprive them of sunlight so as to retain their whiteness and only allow them to take the desired degree of color. Pink or purple asparagus are allowed to grow a few inches above the soil while the green variety is harvested when it is about five inches long. The "American"variety – usually grown in Spain – reaches its full length, a much simpler and cheaper process.

The all-green asparagus has been known since early Antiquity and was a great favorite with the Ancient Romans. Virtually forgotten during the Middle Ages, it reemerged during the Renaissance. Louis XIV was particularly fond of asparagus and La Quintinie, who was in charge of the monarch's kitchen garden, perfected the art of forcing the plants under glass in order to satisfy the royal cravings earlier in the season. During the eighteenth century, growers noticed that, while the whitening process produced vegetables that were more tender, their skins were thick and had to be removed before cooking. Hence the preference for nice, fat asparagus. In the nineteenth century, the horticulturists of Argenteuil made asparagus their specialty and perfected a variety which became generally known by the name of the locality. The same name was used in the Durance Valley, where cultivation also began during the same century. In the 1890s, Auguste Escoffier, *chef de cuisine* at London's Savoy Hotel, whose guests only liked green asparagus tips, urged the growers of Lauris, in the Rhône Valley, to devote themselves to producing this type of plant. At first, only a few agreed but so successful were they that all the rest soon followed suit.

Alain Ducasse's supplier is Robert Blanc, whose family has been producing asparagus since 1870, when his grandfather settled at Villelaure. Little has changed since then, other than the fact that Robert has managed to spread the firm's reputation far and wide for the care he lavishes on this laborious type of cultivation. Blanc's asparagus is hand-picked, sorted spear by spear several times over, trimmed of any parts damaged during the harvest, then shortened and carefully graded. Because he is of a poetic – and roguish – turn of mind, he has given each category a name. The biggest ones are "*bourgeoise*", because somebody once told him that asparagus were bourgeois vegetables, the rest are known respectively as "*demoiselles*" – young ladies, "*fillettes*" – girls, and "*pitchounes*" – little'uns. Each category comes in a short or long version, apart from the *bourgeois*'s which come in three sizes: "Danielle", "Brigade" and "Mireille". They are then tied in bundles and bound with ribbon. The cut ends are soaked in water for 15 minutes to refresh them and ensure that they survive the journey. Given such VIP treatment, asparagus is indeed a regal vegetable!

● WHEAT AND FLOUR

Wheat and flour are such commonplace products that we barely give them a second thought. Nevertheless, wheat has long been the Mediterranean cereal *par excellence*. Even now, those who live around the Mediterranean treat it in quite different ways from their more northerly neighbors, using it to create various types of pasta, couscous and cracked wheat, as well as a rich variety of breads. When Alain Ducasse first came to the Mediterranean, he naturally took a close interest in the ingredients utilized for the pasta, gnocchi and the nine different kinds of bread served at the Louis XV.

Strangely, it is impossible to trace the precise history of the cereal crop, whose cultivation must certainly have coincided with the growth of civilization. It appears that there were three types of wild grasses which gave birth to the main wheat families (today there are hundreds of different varieties). The most primitive was emmer, traces of which have been found among the excavated relics of ancient Middle Eastern civilizations. The other two are soft wheat and hard, or durum, wheat. Wheat and spelt belong to the first family, while the second produces the semolina from which pasta and couscous are made.

Whatever the variety, a grain of wheat consists of several parts of differing nutritional value. The outer husk is removed straight after harvesting, leaving the grain, which is composed of three parts: the bran coat around the kernel (not to be confused with the husk), the kernel or endosperm, which is the flesh of the grain, and the embryo or germ. The bran is rich in fiber, protein, vitamins and mineral salts. The kernel is rich in starch and the characteristic wheat proteins which, when moistened, turn into gluten, and that is what makes the wheat suitable for bread-making (its elasticity allows the dough to rise during fermentation). Wheat germ is the most nutritious part, packed with vitamins and especially fats, although the modern flour industry has attempted to remove it during the milling process, as the fats can turn rancid and produce an unpleasant taste. Since most of the bran has been extracted to make the flour whiter, it would seem that not a great deal of nourishment remains!

The fast-disappearing, traditional flour mills still use millstones rather than metal cylinders for grinding. They also retain the wheat germ and varying proportions of bran, according to whether the end product is white, brown or wholemeal flour. The quality is usually indicated by a number: "types" 45, 55, 65 and so on. Stone-grinding always produces flour of a type superior to 65, while cylinder-ground flour is less than 65. Ducasse buys his flour at the Moulins de la Marne, where they not only continue to use millstones but are also very fastidious about grain supplies. They consistently use the same suppliers, carefully select wheat varieties and analyze samples before taking delivery. Organically-grown wheat must score above average for protein content and in the "Zeleny Sedimentation Test", which measures the bread-making and gluten qualities of wheat flour. The grain is then processed with extreme care: sifted twice, brushed to remove extraneous matter, washed to clean the crease, then brushed again before being stored for 24 hours, having been soaked if necessary to achieve the correct and uniform humidity level. It is then ground on the millstone, which has to be "re-dressed" by hand at least every three months to ensure the surface is rough enough. An arduous task which has caused more than one millstone to be abandoned.

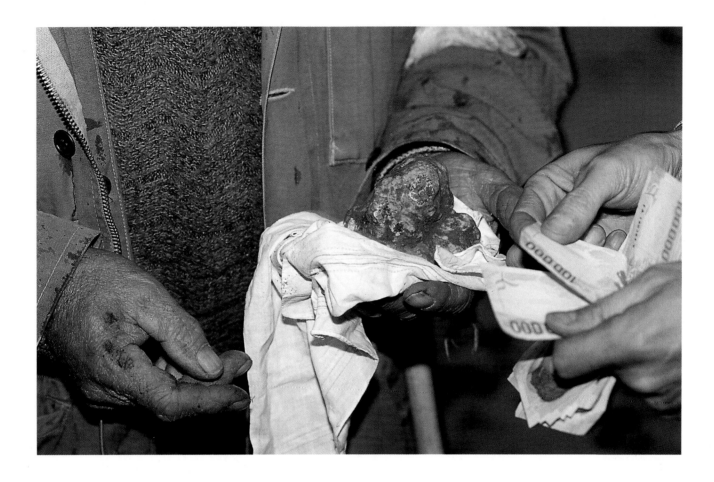

● "TARTUFI DI ALBA"

Alain Ducasse has undeniably made a major contribution to promoting the *tuber magnatum pico*, or Alba truffle, in France. Although it was praised in some nineteenth-century cookbooks, French gourmets had long forgotten how good it could taste. This type of truffle is found almost exclusively in Piedmont, although it also grows in much smaller quantities in several other northern Italian provinces. No one has ever succeeded in cultivating it, or rather in cultivating the species of trees with which truffles live in symbiosis, as has been done for black Périgord truffles. Because of their unique character, Alain Ducasse believes they should be referred to by their Italian name: *tartufi di Alba*.

The truffle is a subterranean fungus of the genus *Tuber*, which most commonly lives in symbiosis with lime trees but also with willows and poplars, particularly in a small area of Piedmont around the towns of Asti, Alba and Mondovi, also the home of some of Italy's finest wines. The first *tartufi* appear in early autumn, and during October, November and December, visitors to the region should not be surprised to see the inhabitants of the Langhe walking about with a distinctly conspiratorial air. They have every reason to do so, since the tubers fetch a high price, usually double that of the black truffle. *Tartufi* are rounded and irregularly shaped, their average diameter varying between one and six inches. The skin is smooth, the color of old ivory, changing from pale beige when first picked and yellowing with age. The flesh is pinkish beige with paler, almost white veins, and gives off a unique fragrance. Strong, intoxicating, irresistible, and extremely complex, so much so that it is hard to define – a blend of garlic, mushrooms and mature parmesan cheese.

Tartufi di Alba are only eaten raw: too much heat spoils the texture and flavor. By contrast, when they are finely minced over a dish containing fatty ingredients, such as oil, butter and egg yolk, usually combined with starch, the gentle heat these emit helps to enhance and fix the flavor of the truffles. While Italians also serve truffles with eggs and raw meat, the tubers are traditionally combined with pasta, gnocchi and *risotto*. But a number of variations are possible based on these traditions.

Digging for truffles is regulated by law. Anyone can search for truffles but, like hunting and fishing, it requires a permit. There are hundreds of diggers in the Langhe. Obviously, they cannot consume all the truffles they find themselves, so they take them to market, where the *tartufi* are bought by brokers who supply shops and restaurants, or arrange for them to be exported. Alain Ducasse purchases his truffles from *Signore* Rossano of Vezza d'Alba, one of Italy's leading *tartufi* suppliers, who only sells exceptional specimens to an exclusive clientele. Ducasse claims, with some justification, that because he buys for his various restaurants, he is the world's biggest consumer of *Tartufi di Alba*.

● SEA BASS FROM THE MEDITERRANEAN

The sea bass is one of the noblest of all fish, but when Alain Ducasse talks about sea bass he means the *loup* or Mediterranean bass, rather than the Atlantic variety. This is also a very fine fish, but in his opinion, the Mediterranean bass has much more character. He likes big fish which can be cut into thick, succulent fillets and he prefers those caught with hook and line. Farmed fish are definitely out: it is like comparing a Boeing 747 and Concorde: one is a great heavy, hulking thing while the other is slender and full of vitality. Besides, if he were offered only farmed bass, he would opt for a humbler wild fish. Ducasse has many ways of preparing sea bass: broiled or roasted, but now considers it is best steamed, as plain as possible.

The bass likes very oxygenated water. It swims close to the coast where breakers and rollers stir up the sea. A voracious predator – not for nothing is it called the loup, or wolf – it feeds on small fish, crabs and squid. Still the best way to fish for bass is to drag a baited hook or a long-line paternoster (a line to which several baited hooks are attached) through the water. Bass can sometimes be caught with nets, if they do not escape before the nets are hauled, but they do not stand up well to this method of fishing. Crammed between all the other fish at the bottom of the net, they suffocate and drown. On the other hand, caught with a hook with live bait such as a sardine, mackerel or bogue, it tries to escape and, in its efforts to spit out the hook, it regurgitates its stomach contents, so there is no need to clean the fish immediately, which means it keeps much better.

In Nice, the sea bass is truly the king of the fishes. It loves the steep coastline here and, even where there are beaches, it swims very close to the shore, while at Sète on the Languedoc coast

it manages to find its way into ponds where the water is not of the same quality. Bass are more likely to be found near the mouths of little coastal rivers, provided they are completely unpolluted, since the fish cannot tolerate dubious water. They are fished from traditional Mediterranean "*pointus*", small, tapered boats barely 20 feet long, whose low draft allows them to sail very close inshore, even along the beaches, to reach the bass's favorite spots. Catches are better in autumn and winter. In summer the waters are too hot and bathers create far too much disturbance. Alex, the fisherman from whom Alain Ducasse prefers to buy, has a soft spot for this wily fish, far too intelligent to let itself be hooked easily. He takes his *pointu*, *Barabas*, to the mouths of the rivers Paillon or Magnan, which are now underground, and baits his paternoster with whole, live fish, with the hooks above their heads, and leaves it to trail in the water. If conditions are right, he has a very good chance of bringing home the coveted bass. He has succeeded in catching specimens three feet long, weighing between 15 ½ and 17 ½ pounds and nearly thirty years old. And even if the catch is unexceptional, he may come home

with a spiny lobster fit for a king, a few red mullet or a superb John Dory. As it is less than a quarter of a mile from Nice harbor to cours Saleya where his mother sells the fish he catches, the goods on offer could hardly be fresher, although, of course, sea bass must be left to "rest" for 24 hours before eating.

● TURBOT FROM BRITTANY

In the old days, turbot was one of the crowning glories of aristocratic tables. All the great classical chefs devised clever and highly complex turbot recipes. Alain Ducasse sees it as the obvious choice for inclusion on the menu of his Paris restaurant. As a tribute to the traditions of the past, he has set himself the task of bringing turbot up to date. He considers that the best turbot are fished from the Atlantic, especially around Brittany, the French capital's traditional source of supply. Naturally, he will only accept fish caught by small boats, since these days, turbot can equally well be the product of a fish farm. Which is not the same thing at all. Only wild fish can reach a respectable weight, enabling them to be cut into thick slices, perfect for roasting or cooking *en cocotte*. Fish farmers, meanwhile, specialize in small specimens which are much cheaper to produce and easier to sell. In the past, turbot was only ever cooked whole, inspiring the invention of the *turbotière*, a fish kettle specially designed to hold its lozenge-shaped body – but modern cooks are perfectly happy to prepare it in pieces, but still on the bone which lends the flesh its distinctive flavor. For this reason, some chefs prefer to cut up a smaller fish in order to obtain slices that are not too thin, the size of the slices depending on the size of the fish.

Breton turbot are fished all along the coast at depths ranging between 16 and 1,000 feet. They are fairly relaxed fish that like the sandy seabed where they hunt by day, while at night they trap their prey in deep water. Turbot are found close offshore from May to mid-September, when the sea is warm and full of other species, such as the small fish, crabs and shellfish on which they feed. Turbot are usually trawled, although some are caught in the ledger lines laid to catch other fish, such as conger eel and skate. However, catches of turbot are jeopardized by the presence of barrages of nets used for intensive fishing. Supplies are uncertain and it is impossible for a restaurant like Alain Ducasse's to rely on one single supplier. The most practical solution is to use a broker who collects fish from various crews. Ducasse buys from Gallen, a wholesale fish merchant based at Concarneau.

Once the turbot is hauled aboard, it must be carefully cleaned and bled, in sea water, to avoid the blood clots that might spoil the pure white flesh. It must also be scrupulously scrubbed to remove the mucus-like layer covering the skin, which would otherwise adversely

affect the flavor, either during transportation or while cooking. What gourmets appreciate most of all is the density of the turbot's flesh, although a freshly-caught turbot must be allowed to rest for 24 hours before cooking.

● LAMB FROM THE PYRENEES

Alain Ducasse loves lamb. Perhaps he acquired the taste during his childhood in south-western France, sandwiched between Pauillac and the Pyrenees. Perhaps it was during his time in the Mediterranean region where the sheep is the number one source of meat. Or maybe it was in Paris, with its fondness for a good plain leg of lamb or cut-lets cleverly prepared by gourmet chefs. No matter, the taste is there, inspiring him to create new recipes. Ducasse searched long and hard to discover the region most likely to provide good lamb of consistent quality. He now believes he has found, in the Pyrenees, the kind of animal to meet his demands: expertly slaughtered, with a flawless thoracic cavity, and rapidly chilled so that the fat has not had time to sweat. As well as their place of origin, the lambs display all the virtues of a genuinely first-class product.

They are divided into three categories. Those slaughtered at the age of 45 days will only have been fed on their mothers' milk. The meat is so tender that it is almost limp and even when raw is a delicate shade of pink. It must always be cooked to the medium stage. The second category is the *agneau blanc* (also known as *laiton*), so called because of its white fat, which is slaughtered at the age of 100 to 120 days. Lambs between four and six months are called *broutards*, or grazing lambs. Because they feed on grass, their flesh is denser but retains the flavors acquired in the pastures. This is especially true of *prés-salés* (salt meadow) lambs.

Pyrenean suckling lambs are traditionally reared for Easter. In the Basque Country and the Béarn region, they are born between mid-November and the end of May. They have to be slaughtered before the age of 45 days, when their live weight is between 26 and 33 pounds, and the carcass weighs a little under 22 pounds, an ideal weight for carving. The early removal of the lambs allows the ewes to keep their milk, which is used for making cheese, for these are the Basque Country's milk-producers. The lambs born to the Manech ewes with their ginger or black faces and big, curly horns, and the Basco-Béarnaises, which live on the high mountain pastures, are only fed on their mothers' milk, never on milk from unknown sources. No chemical additives for these

animals. In winter, the ewes eat hay and in the summer they graze in the high mountain pastures. Axuria (the word means "lamb" in Basque) is a cooperative founded in the early Eighties. It now has around 230 members and fully guarantees the "traceability" of its livestock. This rather barbaric new buzz word simply means that the cooperative knows the pedigree of each animal, the conditions under which it has been reared, and the name of the breeder. Hence, any carcass leaving the excellent abattoir at Mauléon, which complies to the letter with all the European hygiene regulations, can be identified down to the last detail. The quality is confirmed by the award of a quality label.

● CITRUS FRUITS FROM MENTON

For Alain Ducasse, the lemon and all citrus fruits are the other "signature" of the Mediterranean. The lemon tree is the third part of the trilogy which also comprises the olive and cypress trees. All year round, the scent of lemon blossom pervades the air and, as you brush past the leaves, they, too, give off a subtle perfume. The Mediterranean coast would not be the same without this dark and fragrant foliage, studded with bright splashes of yellow, orange and pale green. And what a pleasure it is to pick the fruit straight from the tree! Ducasse likes them because they combine three basic tastes: acidity, sweetness and bitterness. All they lack is salt, which can easily be added for use in non-dessert dishes. And what riches they offer for desserts! Every part of the citrus fruit, flesh, juice and rind, is edible and each has it own distinctive flavor.

The genus *Citrus* came from distant Asia. The orange and mandarin originated in China, the lemon in Kashmir and the grapefruit in Malaysia. Arab adventurers first came across them in India and brought them to the Middle East. In Antiquity, the only known citrus fruit was the citron and it was only during the Middle Ages that Italy and Provence discovered the bitter oranges and lemons grown in Palestine. Medieval Hyères was one of the main ports from which Crusaders set sail for the Holy Land and it would have been through here that the fruit was introduced to the western end of the north Mediterranean coast. The citrus orchards of the Côte d'Azur date back many hundreds of years and were renowned until the last century, when, for economic reasons, they fell into decline. The orchards were situated at the northernmost limit of the region best suited to their cultivation, and were exposed to frost. It was cheaper to cultivate oranges and lemons in newly-conquered Algeria. Nevertheless, the mandarins and oranges of Antibes and Nice and the lemons of Menton enjoyed a very good reputation among connoisseurs. Today, the region still produces fruit of recognized quality. Although the oranges ripen late and have a slightly sour taste, rather like the Maltese variety, the lemons are very sweet, much like those from Amalfi. The local clementines, belonging to rather older and less productive varieties than elsewhere, have a delicate aroma and are great favorites with confectioners.

When people in Menton talk about lemons, they are bound to mention the name of Séverin Capra. His parents were vegetable growers, but he decided to devote his efforts to lemons and create a citrus tree nursery. This was a brave move in the immediate postwar years.

No tree nursery had existed since 1925, but lemon trees were traditionally regarded locally as a good way of staying out of debt. As they blossomed and bore fruit throughout the year (the only plant to do so, apart from rosemary), anyone in need of money only had to take a basket, pick a few lemons, then sell them in the market to raise the necessary cash. However, almost all the trees were destroyed by heavy frosts, and urban development was constantly pushing back the boundaries of the orchards on the precipitous slopes of the hinterland. Undaunted, Séverin Capra set up in business, sowed his seeds, and waited the necessary five or six years for the shrubs to produce their first fruits – afterwards, the yield doubles every two years reaching between 45 and 110 pounds of fruit after about 15 years. While earning a living as a landscape gardener, he gradually developed and expanded his nursery. He now cultivates around 1,000 trees on two and a half acres of land, tending them all by hand. Often the terrain is too steep to be tackled by a motor cultivator which can only be used on level terraces. He concentrates on lemon trees because they are easier – the ripe fruit does not fall from the branches – and the soil is just right for them. He usually grafts them onto mandarin trees, making them much more productive. Cultivating lemons is a pleasure: the more you pick, the more they grow – provided, of course, the frost stays away. But Monsieur Capra is philosophical and treats his trees parsimoniously, so that his fruit is of a consistent standard. He believes nature knows best and it is also one way to destroy vermin, provided the plants are not killed stone dead, of course. Pruned right back, they are rejuvenated and start all over again. Some of them survive for centuries and can reach an age of 250.

Vegetables

Vegetables

Often regarded as food for invalids or convalescents, vegetables have largely been neglected by exponents of *haute cuisine* and good, plain cooks alike, who have simply served them as a garnish. Both culinary styles offered little more than one way to cook them, namely *"à l'anglaise"*, in other words, plain boiled, probably the worst possible method imaginable. August Escoffier's *Guide Culinaire*, devotes only 50 out of its 900 pages to vegetables! It may simply be because, for so long, vegetables have formed the foundation of working-class fare, albeit with a somewhat limited range in certain regions, and hence were not considered sufficiently "distinguished" to grace more illustrious tables.

● DISCOVERY

Although a southerner himself, when Alain Ducasse joined Roger Vergé at the Moulin de Mougins, the Mediterranean South proved a revelation to him. Throughout Provence there is a veritable vegetable cult. He only had to see the stalls in the Forville market in Cannes, or Nice's cours Saleya: the little lettuces, the wild herbs picked in the hinterland, the crates overflowing with greens gathered the evening before, kept chilled overnight – in the cellar, under the arbor, but never, ever in the refrigerator – and brought to market completely fresh. This was only the beginning for the young *chef de partie*; when his turn came to preside over the kitchen, he would take the matter much further. Above all, it was while working with Alain Chapel that he became convinced by that great chef's insistence that only superlative products were good enough. Once he became his own master, he immediately applied Chapel's philosophy. Free to go where he pleased, follow his own whims and make his own choices, he set out to explore the Mediterranean region and was immediately captivated. In Italy, he found the fondness for vegetables even more pronounced than in Provence. There, he discovered new ways of preparing them and, more importantly, products as yet unknown in France. The quest would continue as he moved through the region as *chef de cuisine* at L'Amandier in Mougins, and later at the Hôtel Juana's Terrasse restaurant at Juan-les-Pins, and the various restaurants at Monte Carlo's Hôtel de Paris.

● A HOMAGE TO VEGETABLES

The search culminated in Ducasse's efforts in the kitchens of the Louis XV at the Hôtel de Paris. While, at first sight, the vegetables might have seemed modest fare, they actually demanded enormous amounts of time and loving care. They had to be of the highest quality and required numerous skilled staff to prepare and present them to the best advantage. This was the only restaurant where diners could enjoy the unheard-of luxury of several delicious vegetables. Having taken over in Monte Carlo, Alain Ducasse could finally indulge his passion. Pulling out all the stops, he soon offered diners his "Jardins de Provence", an all-vegetable, but not vegetarian, menu, changing with the seasons. For once, roles were reversed and green vegetables occupied center stage, sometimes seasoned with a meat *jus* or shavings of crispy bacon, or accompanied by an egg. There was no room for restraint, rules or regulations. It was simply about the sheer pleasure of exploiting the wealth of scents, flavors and textures fresh from the garden.

Of course, this kind of exercise can only succeed using the very finest produce. There is no question of making do with any old vegetable, forced at breakneck speed in some obscure nursery. If they are to taste anything other than bland and insipid, if their texture is to resemble anything other than cotton wool or blotting paper, vegetables must be grown in soil and at the season that nature intended. There are still plenty of places where small vegetable growers and country-dwellers from the surrounding area bring their own produce to market. They are the

best source of supply – better still if the locality happens to be the Mediterranean coast. Their vegetables really do taste different. Alain Ducasse chooses to stock up almost daily from these producers, and has even remained faithful to some whom he first encountered while working with Roger Vergé.

As soon as he discovered La Bastide at Moustiers, Alain Ducasse began to dream of creating a kitchen garden there. Little by little, with the aid of his trusty gardener Benoît Bauvallet, the dream became reality, enabling guests at this little Provençal house to sample pleasures that have become all too rare. The delight of tasting vegetables only just picked, right at the moment of ripening, of a variety cultivated specifically for its flavor and perfume and not for its resistance to shocks, dramatic temperature changes or premature rot. The satisfaction of savoring a vegetable virtually *au naturel*, seasoned only with herbs grown alongside it. But also the simple pleasure of breathing in the fragrance of leaves in the sunshine, or the smell of the soil after its evening watering; or seeing lettuces swollen with milky sap, peas and beans on the branch, tomatoes reddening beneath the leaves, a perfect image of health and vitality.

● A PASSION FOR EXPERIMENTATION

However, Alain Ducasse did not only find exceptional products along the Mediterranean. He also discovered a genuine passion for vegetables and previously unknown methods of preparation, devised to bring out the best in them and transform them into a gastronomic treat. They could be pounded, as in *pistou* or *tapenade*; raw and left whole, as in *anchoïade provençale*, *bagna cauda* – a hot version of *anchoïade* – and Italian *pinzimonio*. Peppers, mushrooms and artichokes could be preserved in oil, or dried and preserved like the sun-dried

tomatoes of Sicily. Zucchini could be broiled, steamed or roasted. One day, while chatting with a woman shopping at the same market stall, Alain Ducasse learned the recipe for "*tourte pasqualine*". In this springtime dish, raw Swiss card, artichokes, fava beans, peas and baby onions seasoned with borage and marjoram are steamed under a fine layer of pastry, concentrating their flavors and preserving their texture and character right to the last mouthful. Another day, he heard about *tourte aux blettes*, sweet Swiss chard pie, a typical dessert from Nice.

Armed with this new knowledge, the chef embarked on experiments of his own. He might cook each vegetable separately in a skillet or stew pot to isolate and concentrate the flavor, or create "raw and cooked" pairings, which, he claims: "combine on the same plate to show how heat can transform the taste of food quite astonishingly: a raw tomato stuffed with preserved tomato; a thinly-sliced, raw artichoke heart with another browned in oil: raw, shredded basil leaves used to season a fillet of bass sprinkled with more basil, fried whole". Other fascinating new recipes were inspired by rustic styles of cooking which manage to create quite delectable

dishes from the humblest ingredients, making use of pods and leaves which are usually thrown away but whose flavors are often more intense. For example, fava bean pods with their cotton wool-like insides make a delicious, creamy soup. And, if the vegetables are really outstanding, why not dare to serve them *au naturel?*

● TRANSFERRING THE EXPERIMENT

Nevertheless, the experiments that worked so well in the South of France were hard to reproduce elsewhere. When he opened his Paris restaurant, Alain Ducasse hoped to draw on his Mediterranean experience with vegetables but this proved problematic. There was the problem of finding the right vegetable suppliers. The Île-de-France is still a great vegetable growing region but most of its products do not have the same flavor as those grown on the shores of the Mediterranean, and some are simply unobtainable. Parisians know nothing of bitter salad leaves (even though market stalls overflow with cultivated arugula) or zucchini flowers, and can one honestly say that good tomatoes can be found in the French capital? There was also a cultural problem. More than any others, Parisians are heirs to the great culinary tradition that accords the place of honor to meat, fish and game, and old habits die hard. It was the perfect opportunity for Alain Ducasse to continue his experiments and find ways of communicating his enthusiasm.

Recipes

Mediterranean Vegetable Pithiviers with Black Taggiasca Olives and Tomato Syrup

BY ALAIN DUCASSE

4 SERVINGS

FROM THE MARKET
- **2 zucchini flowers**
- **Olive oil**
- **Salt**

Puff pastry
- **2 cups (350 g) flour**
- **3 ½ sticks (350 g) unsalted butter**
- **1 teaspoon (5 g) salt**

Pithiviers
- **3 sweet red peppers**
- **3 sweet green peppers**
- **Olive oil**
- **5 black peppercorns**
- **4 garlic cloves**
- **12 tomatoes**
- **1 sprig thyme**
- **4 green zucchini**
- **4 ounces (100 g) black tapenade**
- **1 egg yolk**

Prepare the puff pastry two days in advance. Work 1 stick (100g) butter with a spatula until soft and easy to spread. Blend the flour, salt and ½ cup (12.5 cl) water to create an even dough. Knead the softened butter into the dough and leave to rest for 30 minutes.

On a lightly floured work surface, roll the dough out into the shape of a cross. Place the remaining butter in the center. Fold the dough over the butter to form an envelope. Roll the dough into a rectangle, so that the length is three times the width. Fold the rectangle into three and leave it to rest in the refrigerator for 6 hours.

Place the dough on the floured work surface and give it a quarter-turn. Roll it out in the same way as before and fold it into three. Leave it to rest in the refrigerator for 12 hours. Repeat the "turn, roll, fold" process for a third time, giving the dough a quarter-turn. Leave to rest for 6 hours before repeating the process for the fourth and final time, and leave to rest for 12 hours.

Prepare the pepper and tomato confit, preferably the day before. Place the red and green peppers under the grill, as close as possible to the heat source and leave until the skins blacken, turning regularly. Encase the peppers in saran wrap and place them under cold running water: this makes them easier to skin. Remove the skins with the aid of a small knife. Remove the stalk, deseed and cut the flesh into quarters. Arrange the pieces in a large skillet, making sure that they are lying as flat as possible, and drizzle with olive oil. Season with salt and peppercorns and add 2 garlic cloves, unpeeled but lightly crushed with the blade of a knife. Leave to simmer very gently over a very low heat for about an hour.

Preheat the oven on its very lowest setting. To make the tomato confit, plunge the tomatoes in boiling water for a few seconds, then pass them immediately under cold, running water. Remove the skins, then cut into quarters and deseed. Arrange on a baking sheet or large ovenproof dish. Drizzle lightly with olive oil. Peel and crush two garlic cloves and sprinkle over the tomatoes. Remove the leaves from the sprig of thyme and sprinkle over the tomatoes, then place them in the oven and roast for 2 hours.

Prepare the zucchini: preheat the oven to 245°F (120°C; gas mark ¼). Wash the zucchini and remove the skins together with a thin layer of flesh. Arrange the zucchini ribbons on a baking sheet, drizzle lightly with olive oil and roast in the oven for 10 minutes. Leave to cool.

Assemble the pithiviers: using 4 pastry cutters, 4 inches (10 cm) in diameter, as templates, arrange a layer of tomatoes inside each circle and spread with *tapenade*. Cover with a layer of zucchini, spread with *tapenade* and cover with a layer of red peppers. Spread with more *tapenade* and finish with a layer of green peppers. Reserve 5 slivers of tomato for the tomato syrup.

Roll out the dough and cut it into 8 rounds, 5 inches (12 cm) in diameter. With the help of a large spatula, transfer the pithiviers to the first four rounds of dough. Remove the metal cutters and cover the vegetables with the remaining four rounds of dough. Moisten the edges and press them firmly together, then use a knife to create the traditional pithiviers scalloped edges. With the point of a knife, decorate the tops with half-moon shapes and pierce a small hole in the center of each pithiviers to allow the steam to escape. Mix the egg yolk in a cup with a tablespoon of water.

Tomato syrup
- **5 tomatoes**
- **3 leaves fresh basil**
- **2 garlic cloves**
- **10 black olives**

Special utensils
- **4 round cutters, 4 inches (10 cm) in diameter, to use as templates**
- **1 cookie cutter, 5 inches (12 cm) in diameter**

● Peel the peppers. Remove the stalks and deseed, then cut the flesh into quarters.

● Prepare the tomato confit with garlic, a sprig of thyme and a little olive oil.

● Using a mandolin, carefully remove the skin of the zucchini with just a little flesh attached.

● If you do not have a mandolin, simply use a sharp kitchen knife.

● Using round cutters, 4 inches (10 cm) in diameter, as templates, arrange the tomatoes, tapenade and zucchini in layers.

● Continue with layers of red pepper, tapenade and green peppers.

● Roll the dough thinly on a lightly floured work surface.

● Replace the cookie cutter with a round of dough. Use a small knife to create a scalloped edge.

Brush the tops with this glaze, making sure it does not run down the sides. Leave to stand in a cool place for at least an hour.

Make the tomato syrup: plunge the tomatoes in boiling water for a few seconds, then pass them immediately under cold, running water. Remove the skins, then cut into quarters and deseed. Transfer the tomato flesh to a saucepan, add the basil and the garlic cloves, peeled and crushed. Heat through over a low flame for about 5 minutes, then pass through a chinois (or fine sieve). Crush the 5 reserved pieces of tomato confit and heat them through with a little water to produce aromatic tomato juice, then mix the contents of the saucepan with the sieved raw tomatoes and pass again through the chinois. Cut the black olives into slivers with a small knife and discard the pits. Stir the olive slivers into the tomato syrup.

● With the point of a knife, pierce a hole in the center of each pithiviers.

● Heat the tomato pulp, basil leaves and garlic over a low heat for five minutes.

● Crush 5 slivers of tomato confit and heat in a little water.

● Place the black olives on a work surface and cut the flesh into slivers.

Bake the pithiviers: preheat the oven to 350 F (180°C; gas mark 4). Place the pithiviers in the hot oven and cook for 25 minutes until the pastry is golden. As soon as they are done, transfer them to a rack to cool.

Reheat the tomato syrup over a low heat.

While the pithiviers are cooking, wipe the zucchini flowers and cut them in half lengthwise. Heat a little olive oil in a skillet, add the zucchini flowers and fry them for 1 ½ minutes on each side. Season lightly with salt.

To serve, spoon a little tomato syrup onto each plate and add the pithiviers. Place half a zucchini flower alongside. Pour some tomato syrup into the hole in the top of each pithiviers and serve.

Wine suggestion: a rosé, such as a 1995 "Rosé d'une nuit" from the Clos Marfisi estate in southern Corsica.

● Stir the slivered olives into the tomato syrup.

● Cut the zucchini flowers in half lengthwise.

● Reheat the tomato syrup over a low heat.

● Spoon a little tomato syrup with olive slivers onto each plate.

66 THE "TAGGIASCA" OLIVE (NAMED AFTER THE LITTLE TOWN OF TAGGIA, INLAND FROM SAN REMO) IS THE SAME AS THE LITTLE "*CAILLETIER*" OLIVE FROM NICE. ITS COLOR CHANGES FROM GREEN TINGED WITH PINK TO A DEEP, ALMOST BLACK, PURPLE WHEN FULLY RIPE. 99

CONTENTS

●

● Alain Ducasse ●
Mediterranean Vegetable Pithiviers with Black Taggiasca Olives and Tomato Syrup

In this recipe, Alain Ducasse combines puff pastry, one of his favorite classic recipes, and a filling that encapsulates the essential flavors of the Mediterranean, like a *ratatouille* whose ingredients are separated by a layer of *tapenade*. The tomato "syrup" with slivered olives echoes the theme of the filling, creating two different taste experiences inside and outside the pithiviers. Steamed inside their puff pastry case, the flavors of the vegetables are developed to the full and burst forth as soon as the crust is broken.

● Franck Cerutti ●
San Remo-style Salt Cod and Mesclun with Fried Baby Squid and Croûtons

Cod, wind-dried on sticks, is very widely used in Nice and in Italy. For this *brandade*, it is absolutely essential to use top-quality olive oil, since inferior oil tastes unpleasantly woody when heated. Olives add an interesting touch to the blend and interplay of textures, as do the *supions* (baby squid) and croûtons in the *mesclun*. This traditional Mediterranean combination of salad leaves should include bitter herbs (in winter, Cerutti uses dandelion leaves) to heighten the flavor of the dish.

• Jean-Louis Nomicos •
Potato Millefeuille with Black Olives, Spider Crab Meat and Coral Vinaigrette

Slivers of olives, slipped between very fine layers of potato, not only add flavor (they are blanched first to make them sweeter and, more importantly, so that they do not overwhelm the other ingredients) but also an unexpected smoothness to contrast with the very crunchy potatoes. The spider crab meat, also very sweet, is seasoned with a discreet touch of olive oil flavored only with a few drops of lemon juice, as is the vinaigrette made with shellfish *jus*.

• Sylvain Portay •
Zucchini Ravioli with Olives, Marinated Tomatoes, Olive Oil and Green Onions

Olives feature in this recipe in three different textures and three different flavors providing three distinctive taste experiences. Their flesh appears in the stuffing; *tapenade* (olives puréed with other ingredients) is blended into the ravioli dough; finally, olive oil is a basic element of the tomato marinade and the sauce. The zucchini filling and the marinated tomatoes lend freshness to this dish of pure Monegasque inspiration.

• Jean-François Piège •
Olive-stuffed Squab with Olive and Cep Sauce

For Jean-François Piège, olives evoke his childhood. In this classically-inspired recipe – a variation of pigeon *sur canapé* – he uses it in two guises. The flesh of the olives, which complements poultry and red meat so well, lends flavor to the stuffing and sauce. Olive oil is used to cook the squab for the same reasons, but also because it seals the meat to perfection. He chooses Taggiasca olives for the subtle variations in taste according to when they are harvested, and because they enhance rather than mask the other flavors.

• Alessandro Stratta •
Calf's Cheeks with Olives and Swiss Chard

In this recipe, olives are used in a highly traditional way: to lend piquancy to the pan juices and in the form of oil to bind them. The olives and the oil should both be mildly flavored so as not to overpower the delicate taste of the veal, gnocchi and Swiss chard, but at the same time strong enough to add a distinctive and elegant touch to a dish inspired by the traditional *daube niçoise aux olives* (meat braised in wine with olives).

San Remo-style Salt Cod and Mesclun with Fried Baby Squid and Croûtons

BY FRANCK CERUTTI

Seven days before the meal, soak the salt cod in a bowl of cold water. In winter, leave the bowl in the open air. In summer, put it in the refrigerator. Change the water every day. (Salt cod gives off rather a strong smell).

When you are ready to cook, drain the fish. Place it in a saucepan of cold water, add salt, then poach over a low heat for 15 minutes, but do not allow it to come to a boil.

Wash the potatoes and place them in another saucepan of cold water. Add salt, then boil for 25 minutes. Peel the 2 garlic cloves. Warm the olive oil with the garlic. Rinse and dry the parsley and coarsely chop the leaves. Pit the olives.

When the fish is cooked, drain off the water. Skin, fillet and flake the flesh. Drain and peel the potatoes. Press them through a sieve or a potato ricer.

Prepare a *bain-marie:* place the fish and potatoes in a stainless steel bowl, or a heat-resistant salad bowl. Place the bowl over the *bain-marie*. Work the mixture with a spatula, while pouring in the warm olive oil in a continuous stream.

Prepare the garnish: heat the oven to its very lowest setting. Rinse the *supions* (baby squid) under cold running water, separate the heads from the bodies, and remove the entrails and transparent cartilage. Cut off the tentacles on a level with the eyes. Wash the bodies and tentacles, then dry them and leave them on a clean cloth.

Wash and dry the salad leaves. Squeeze the lemon. Prepare the dressing with the olive oil, 1-2 tablespoons of lemon juice, salt and pepper. Peel the garlic clove, cut in half and degerm. Rub the baguette with garlic then cut it into large *croûtons*. Arrange them on a baking sheet and leave them to dry out in the oven.

Heat the frying oil to 350°F (180°C). Fry the squid in small batches. Cover the pan to avoid spitting. Fry the squid for a few minutes until golden. Remove them from the pan and drain on absorbent paper.

Just before serving, add the coarsely chopped parsley and olive to the brandade. Arrange it in neat circles on the plates.

Dress the salad with lemon dressing and arrange it beside the brandade. Garnish with croûtons and fried squid. Serve immediately.

4 SERVINGS

- 1 generous pound (500 g) dried salt cod, cut from the middle of the fish
- 9 ounces (250 g) yellow-fleshed potatoes, such as Mona Lisa
- 2 garlic cloves
- 6 tablespoons (10 cl) olive oil
- 4 sprigs flat-leaf parsley
- 16 "cailletier" olives from the Nice region
- Salt

GARNISH

- 18 ounces (500 g) pistes (baby squid 2 inches (5 cm) long)
- 11 ounces (300 g) mesclun (mixed Provençal salad leaves)
- 3 tablespoons olive oil
- 1 lemon
- 1 garlic clove
- 1 baguette
- Oil for frying
- Salt
- Freshly ground pepper

Wine suggestion: a red AOC Côtes de Provence from the Domaine de Saint-Ser, or a white AOC Côtes de Provence, Domaine de la Courtade, îles de Porquerolles.

Potato Millefeuille with Black Olives, Spider Crab Meat and Coral Vinaigrette

BY JEAN-LOUIS NOMICOS

Prepare the tomato confit: peel and deseed the tomatoes. Cut 3 tomatoes into quarters. Arrange them on a baking sheet. Sprinkle them with salt, pepper and sugar (using equal amounts of salt and sugar), drizzle with olive oil, add a crushed garlic clove and a sprig of thyme and roast in the oven at its very lowest setting.

Prepare the spider crabs: fill a stew pot with 5 quarts (5 l) water, adding all the crab stock ingredients. Bring to a rolling boil and cook the spider crabs over a high heat for 10 minutes. Drain and leave the crabs to cool on a rack. Shell the crabs, reserving the coral. Reserve half the claws and shells for the crab *jus*.

Make a crab *jus* to use in the vinaigrette. Peel and mince the scallion. Peel and mince the garlic cloves. Peel the fresh ginger. Heat 1 tablespoon olive oil in a saucepan. Add the reserved claws and shells. Fry to soften them over a low heat for 5 minutes, stirring constantly. Add the garlic, scallion, tomato, ginger and all the seasonings. Add the chicken stock and simmer for 20 minutes. Pass though a chinois (fine sieve) then return to the pan and reduce to a quarter of the volume.

Finely dice the 3 remaining tomatoes. Place them in a colander, season with salt and pepper and leave them to drain and continue preparing the other ingredients.

Cut the olives into slivers. Place them in a small saucepan of cold water, bring to a boil, then drain and refresh. Repeat the same process once more.

Peel and wash the potato. Slice very thinly, using the grooved blade of a Japanese mandolin. Arrange half the potato slices on a buttered, nonstick baking sheet. Decorate each slice with 5 slivers of olive, then cover with the remaining slices. Cover with buttered baking parchment and lay another baking sheet on top to flatten the potatoes. Bake in the oven for 15 minutes at 325°F (160°C; gas mark 3), then leave the potatoes to dry out on a rack.

Finish making the vinaigrette: crush the coral from the spider crabs with a fork. Add 2 tablespoons lemon juice, 1 teaspoon balsamic vinegar, salt, pepper and crab *jus* and mix with 3 tablespoons olive oil to create a vinaigrette.

Season the spider crab meat with a little olive oil, 1 tablespoon lemon juice, salt and pepper. Coarsely chop the tomato confit and mix with the drained, diced tomatoes. Add 4 shredded basil leaves.

Assemble the millefeuille: arrange a layer of spider crab meat on each plate and top with alternating layers of olive-studded potatoes and tomato confit. Sprinkle with vinaigrette and a few drops of balsamic vinegar. Garnish with 1 or 2 basil leaves and drizzle a little vinaigrette around the millefeuille.

4 SERVINGS

- 4 female spider crabs, each weighing about 1 ¼ pounds (600 g)
- 6 Roma tomatoes
- Sugar, olive oil
- 1 garlic clove, 1 sprig thyme
- ¼ cup (45 g) black Taggiasca olives
- 1 large Bintje, or other yellow-fleshed, starchy potato
- 1 tablespoon (10 g) clarified unsalted butter (see page 171)
- 3 tablespoons lemon juice
- Vintage Balsamic vinegar
- 12 basil leaves, salt, pepper

SPIDER CRAB STOCK
- 1 ½ ounces (40 g) coarse salt
- 1 sprig lemon balm
- Scant ½ ounce (10 g) black peppercorns
- ¾ cup (20 cl) white vinegar
- 1 bouquet garni
- 1 cup (25 cl) dry white wine
- Pinch Cayenne pepper
- Zest of 1 lemon

VINAIGRETTE
- 1 scallion, 2 garlic cloves
- 1 teaspoon (5 g) fresh ginger, 1 tomato
- 4 pieces lemon zest
- ½ sprig lemon balm
- ½ bay leaf
- 1 sprig fresh thyme
- 2 cups (50 cl) chicken stock

SPECIAL UTENSIL
- 1 Japanese mandolin

Wine suggestion: a dry, fruity white wine from Provence, Cassis Clos Val Bruyère, 1996.

Olive-stuffed Squab with Olive and Cep sauce

BY JEAN-FRANÇOIS PIÈGE

Prepare the garlic confit: place the unpeeled garlic cloves in a small saucepan. Cover them with olive oil. Heat until boiling but not smoking, then leave to simmer for 30-35 minutes. Remove from the heat.

Prepare the squab *jus*: peel the scallions and cut them into thick rings. Lightly crush the garlic cloves. Coarsely chop the squab carcasses and brown in a cast iron pot with 1 tablespoon duck fat. Add the scallions and garlic, fry gently for a few minutes, and then moisten with ½ cup chicken stock, scraping the base of the pan with a spatula. Add the rest of the chicken stock and simmer gently for 1 hour. Pass the *jus* through a chinois (fine sieve).

Prepare the garnish: if you cannot find prickly Laon artichokes, use the round Breton variety. Trim the leaves to create a regular shape around the heart, but do not remove too many leaves. Leave a 3 ½ inch (9 cm) stalk on each one. Roast the artichoke in a cast iron pot with a little olive oil. When they are tender, cut them through from top to bottom and remove the hairy choke. Stuff each artichoke half with half a clove of garlic confit, half an olive and a quarter basil leaf. Secure each one with half a rasher of bacon.

Cook the squabs: place a sprig of fresh thyme and a crushed garlic clove inside each bird, then truss them. According to the amount of breast meat, roast the squabs on a spit or rôtisserie for 12-14 minutes until the meat is pink. Cut off the legs and bone them. Leave the squabs to rest for 10 minutes.

Prepare the stuffing: peel and finely mince the scallions. Mince the ceps. Cut the beef bone marrow, the meat from the legs and the *foie gras* into small dice. Thinly slice the Colona ham (or fat bacon). Coarsely chop the olives. Cut the garlic cloves in half, then in half again. Chop the parsley.
Sauté the marrow and *foie gras* over a high heat for 2 minutes, then drain. Gently fry the scallions and ceps in the fat rendered by the bone marrow and *foie gras*. Moisten with 2 tablespoons of squab *jus*, scraping the base of the pan with a spatula. Transfer the whole mixture to a shallow bowl and stir in the rest of the stuffing ingredients while still hot.

Prepare the sauce: bring the squab *jus* to a boil, bind with the minced livers and hearts of the two squab. Add the tapenade and adjust the seasoning. Finally, add finely diced pitted olives and ceps. Reheat the squabs in the oven.

Fry the artichokes for a few minutes, with the bacon side downwards, to make them slightly crisp. Detach the squab breasts and remove the wing tips. Toast the bread, spread it with stuffing and cook in the oven for 2-4 minutes at 350° (180°C; gas mark 4). Place 2 squab breasts on each slice. Arrange one squab on each plate, with the artichokes on the side. Pour over sauce.

2 SERVINGS

- 2 squabs, each weighing about 1 pound (500 g)
- 2 sprigs fresh thyme
- 1 garlic clove, olive oil
- 2 slices farmhouse bread
- Fine salt, pepper

SQUAB JUS
- 4 ounces (100 g) scallions, 2 garlic cloves
- 3 squab carcasses, plus the wing tips
- Duck fat
- 1 quart (1 l) light chicken stock (see page 130)

OLIVE AND CEP SAUCE
- Livers and hearts of the squabs
- 1 generous ounce (30 g) tapenade (olive purée)
- 10 black Taggiasca olives
- 2 ounces (50 g) ceps

STUFFING
- 1 generous ounce (30 g) garlic confit, 2 ounces (50 g) scallions
- 2 ounces (50 g) ceps
- 2 ounces (50 g) beef bone marrow
- 2 ounces (50 g) raw duck foie gras
- 4 ounces (100 g) Colona or other fat bacon
- 4 ounces (100 g) black Taggiasca olives
- 2 ounces (50 g) squab livers and hearts, minced
- 10 sprigs parsley

GARNISH
- 4 prickly artichokes
- 4 Taggiasca olives
- 2 purple basil leaves
- 4 thin rashers streaky bacon

Wine suggestion: a Rhône Valley red, such as Cornas "Les Ruchets", Colombo, 1989.

Zucchini Ravioli with Olives, Marinated Tomatoes, Olive Oil and Green Onions

BY SYLVAIN PORTAY

Marinate the tomatoes for the garnish: peel the tomatoes, cut them into ¼ inch (0.5 cm) slices and arrange them on a plate. Clean and finely mince the green onions. Season the tomatoes with salt and pepper, drizzle with olive oil and a few drops of sherry vinegar. Sprinkle with snipped green onions and leave to marinate for 3-4 hours.

Prepare the ravioli dough: tip the flour, eggs, a pinch of salt, *tapenade* and 2 tablespoons olive oil into a blender. Using the pastry hook attachment, blend at medium speed to obtain a smooth, even dough. Encase in saran wrap and leave to rest in the refrigerator for at least 2 hours.

Prepare the filling: wash and dry the zucchini. Cook them in a steamer for 10 minutes. Drain and squeeze the zucchini in a cloth to remove the water. Place the zucchini flesh in a salad bowl and mash with a fork while still warm. Blend in the flour, followed by the egg. Shred 6 basil leaves. Peel, degerm and finely mince the garlic clove. Add the Parmesan cheese, basil and garlic to the filling. Season, then add the olives.

Assemble the ravioli: roll out the dough as thinly as possible on a lightly floured work surface. Cut the dough into strips 4 inches (10 cm) wide and 20 inches (50 cm) long. Brush the dough to remove any excess flour. Moisten the edges of each strip with a pastry brush. Place the filling in an icing syringe and place small portions of filling 1 ½ inches (4 cm) apart equidistant from the edges. Fold one long edge firmly over the other so as trap the minimum amount of air around the filling. Press around each portion of filling with the fingers to seal the two layers of dough. Cut into half-moon shapes with a fluted cookie cutter. Transfer the ravioli to a large dish.

Make the sauce: Pour the chicken stock into a skillet, adding the butter and 2 tablespoons olive oil. Reduce over a low heat until the mixture has the consistency of a sauce. Shred 5 basil leaves. Add the olives, basil and *tapenade*.

Bring a large saucepan of water to a boil. Add salt. Add the ravioli, poach for 2 minutes. When they float to the surface, drain and roll them in the sauce. Adjust the seasoning.

Place 3 slices of tomato in the center of each plate. Arrange the ravioli on the bed of tomatoes, cover with sauce and serve immediately.

4 SERVINGS

RAVIOLI DOUGH

- 1 ¾ cups (250 g) flour
- 2 eggs
- 1 teaspoon black olive tapenade
- Olive oil, salt

FILLING

- 7 zucchini (with flowers)
- Generous ¼ cup (30 g) flour, 1 egg
- 6 basil leaves
- 1 garlic clove
- ½ cup (50 g) grated Parmesan cheese
- 30 "cailletier" olives, pitted
- Salt, freshly ground pepper

SAUCE AND GARNISH

- 3 ripe tomatoes, 2 green onions
- Sherry vinegar
- ¾ cup (20 cl) light chicken stock (see page 130)
- ½ stick butter
- 5 basil leaves
- Cailletier olives (3 ½ ounces (60 g) pitted weight)
- 1 teaspoon black olive tapenade
- Salt, freshly ground pepper

SPECIAL UTENSIL

- 1 fluted cookie cutter

Wine suggestion: a white Provençal wine, such as Palette, Château Simone, 1993.

Calf's Cheeks with Olives and Swiss Chard

BY ALESSANDRO STRATTA

Cook the meat: preheat the oven to 300° F (150°C; gas mark 2). Peel the garlic, cut the cloves in half and degerm. Peel the onions and cut them into four.

Season the meat with salt and pepper and coat with flour. Heat 2 tablespoons of the olive oil in a large stockpot, and quickly fry the meat in the hot oil to seal and brown. Add the fennel, carrot, onions and garlic. When the vegetables start to soften, add the butter and leave to caramelize for 10 minutes. Add the white wine, scraping the base of the pan with a spatula. Add the thyme and bay leaf. Cook until the liquid has completely evaporated. Add the chicken stock and bring to a boil. Cover and cook in the oven for 2 hours.

Prepare the garnish: wash the potatoes, lay them on a bed of coarse salt and bake in the oven for 45 minutes at 350°F (180°C; gas mark 4).

Separate the leaves and ribs of the Swiss chard. Rinse and finely shred the leaves. Peel the ribs and cut them diagonally into 1 ½-inch (4 cm) pieces. Bring a saucepan of water to the boil, add salt and the lemon juice, and boil the ribs for 3 to 4 minutes. Drain, refresh in iced water, drain again and reserve.

Peel the potatoes and rub them through a sieve to reduce to a purée. Add the flour and egg yolks, blend thoroughly and roll into a cylinder ¾ inch (2 cm) in diameter. Cut the cylinder into 1-inch (2.5 cm) pieces. Press the pieces gently with the back of a fork to produce a grooved effect and place on a floured work surface.

Heat a pan of water, add salt then add the potato gnocchi. Cook in the boiling water for a minute or two until they float to the surface. Transfer the gnocchi to iced water, then drain and drizzle with a few drops of olive oil.

Heat the veal *jus* and butter in a saucepan. Add the chard ribs and gnocchi. Coat with the sauce and sprinkle with half the Parmesan. Arrange the gnocchi and chard ribs in neat layers in a buttered gratin dish. Drizzle with sauce and sprinkle with the rest of the Parmesan. Brown in the oven at 375°F (190°C; gas mark 5) for 10 minutes.

Plunge the tomatoes into boiling water, then peel and dice.

When the meat is cooked, transfer it to a saucepan. Discard the thyme and bay leaves. Mix the pan juices with the vegetables and strain over the meat. Add a small bowlful of Swiss chard leaf strips, together with the diced tomatoes, olives, basil and sherry vinegar. Simmer for 3 minutes. Drizzle with 2 tablespoons of olive oil.

Arrange the meat on 4 plates, and top with the Swiss chard leaves, diced tomatoes and olives, with the rib gratin and gnocchi on the side. Serve hot.

4 SERVINGS

- 4 calf's cheeks
- 3 garlic cloves
- 2 medium white onions
- 4 tablespoons flour
- 4 tablespoons olive oil
- 3 ounces (80 g) fennel, cut into ½-inch (1 cm) sticks
- 3 ounces (80 g) carrot, cut into ½-inch (1 cm) sticks
- 6 tablespoons (3 ounces; 80 g) unsalted butter
- 1 cup (25 cl) dry white wine
- 6 sprigs thyme
- 2 bay leaves
- 2 quarts (2 l) chicken stock
- Salt, freshly milled pepper

VEGETABLE GARNISH

- 4 waxy potatoes such as Mona Lisa
- Coarse salt
- 1 small bunch Swiss chard
- 1 tablespoon lemon juice
- 1 cup (150 g) flour
- 2 egg yolks, 3 tablespoons (40 g) unsalted butter
- 4 tablespoons veal jus (see page 130)
- 4 tablespoons grated Parmesan cheese
- 2 tomatoes
- ⅔ cup (100 g) Taggiasca olives, pitted
- 2 tablespoons shredded basil
- 2 teaspoons sherry vinegar

Wine suggestion: a white Piedmont wine from Italy, such as Barbara d'Alba. Vignarey, A. Gaja.

Roast Asparagus Sprinkled with Parmesan Cheese, with Savory Beef and Olive Jus and Bone Marrow

BY ALAIN DUCASSE

4 SERVINGS

FROM THE MARKET
- 20 *"bourgeoise"* asparagus spears
- 4 marrow bones
- 8 scallions
- Olive oil
- 1 ½ tablespoons (20 g) unsalted butter
- Generous ⅓ cup (40 g) grated Parmesan cheese
- 48 olives, preserved in oil, pitted
- Freshly ground pepper
- Fine salt
- Mignonette (coarsely ground white) pepper
- Salt

Remove the marrow from the bones, place it in a bowl of cold water with ice cubes, and leave to stand in the refrigerator for 6 hours.

Prepare the beef *jus* : peel and thinly slice the scallions. Peel and crush the garlic clove. Peel and chop the carrot. Heat a little olive oil in a stew pot and fry the cubes of beef over a high heat until they take color. Add the scallions, garlic, parsley stems and carrot. Cover the pot and soften the vegetables over a low heat for 10 minutes. Using a ladle, skim off three-quarters of the fat, then add enough water to half cover the ingredients. Cook, uncovered, until all the liquid has evaporated, then fill with enough water to cover and simmer gently for 1 ½ hours. Pass through a chinois (or fine sieve).

Make the savory beef *jus*. Rinse the pot. Preheat the oven to 225°F (110°C ; gas mark ¼). Heat a little olive oil in the pot and brown the oxtail all round over a high heat. Skim off all the fat, add the wine and cook, uncovered, until reduced by half. Add sufficient beef stock to cover the oxtail. Bring to a boil, cover and cook in the oven for 3 hours. Strain the *jus* through a chinois (or fine sieve); it should be creamy in texture and very aromatic.

Peel the scallions. Place them in a saucepan and cover with olive oil. Cover the saucepan and simmer for 35-40 minutes. Peel the asparagus and trim the spears so that they are 5 inches long. Rinse in cold water and dry with a cloth.

● Choose good, plump "bourgeoise" asparagus.

● Pour the red wine over the oxtail, then add the beef *jus.*

● Lay the asparagus on a flat surface and peel them with a vegetable peeler. Cut the bases at an angle.

● Cook the asparagus in foaming butter, basting regularly with the butter.

Heat a little olive oil in a skillet and add a knob of butter. Place the asparagus in the hot fat and roll them around the skillet so that they are evenly colored. Season with salt and cook for 15 minutes. Test with the point of a knife to check that they are cooked. Sprinkle with Parmesan cheese and remove from the skillet.

Drain the bone marrow and cut each piece in half. Plunge the marrow into boiling, salted water and poach for 5-6 minutes, without allowing the water to boil.

Heat the savory beef *jus,* add the olives, then cover and leave to infuse over a very low heat, without allowing it to boil.

Arrange 3 asparagus spears on each plate, then arrange two more crosswise on top. Drain the marrow and arrange two pieces on each plate. Surround with savory beef and olive *jus,* seasoned with pepper. Sprinkle the marrow with fine salt and *mignonette* (coarsely ground white) pepper.

Beef jus
- 1 ½ pounds (600 g) chuck steak, cut into 2 inch (5 cm) cubes.
- 1 oxtail, cut into five equal chunks
- 2 gray scallions
- 1 garlic clove
- 1 small carrot
- Olive oil
- 5 parsley stems
- 1 scant cup (20 cl) red wine

Wine suggestion : a white Saumur, such as Brézé, Foucault frères, 1995.

● Season the asparagus with fine salt and cook for 15 minutes.

● Just before they finish cooking, sprinkle the asparagus with a little Parmesan cheese.

● Reheat the savory beef *jus* with the pitted olives. Leave to infuse for a few minutes.

● Arrange the bone marrow and scallion beside the asparagus with the beef and olive *jus* alongside.

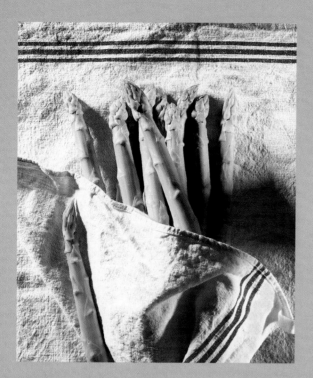

66 THE ASPARAGUS IS A STRANGE VEGETABLE. ONLY A FEW VARIETIES OF THIS PERENNIAL PLANT EXIST BUT THESE CAN APPEAR IN DIFFERENT FORMS ACCORDING TO THE METHOD OF CULTIVATION. ASPARAGUS CAN BE WHITE, PINK, PURPLE OR PROVENÇAL GREEN. 99

CONTENTS

● Alain Ducasse ●
Roast Asparagus Sprinkled with Parmesan Cheese, with Savory Beef and Olive Jus and Bone Marrow

Alain Ducasse likes to bring out the best in green asparagus by serving them with a beef *jus*, offsetting the crispness of the one with the velvety smoothness of the other. Here, the asparagus are seasoned in classic style with finely grated Parmesan cheese. The beef *jus* is highly aromatic, enhanced even further by the addition of olives, creating a counterpoint to the intense flavor of green asparagus. Bone marrow adds richness as well as providing the perfect link between the two highly distinctive main ingredients.

● Franck Cerutti ●
Early Purple Asparagus, Spring Leeks and Late-Season Black Truffles

Leeks – otherwise known as "poor man's asparagus" – are particularly delicious in springtime when the last truffles can still be found. Franck Cerutti likes the idea of combining them with the real thing, in this case the relatively rare purple asparagus, typical of the Nice region and the Ligurian coast. The truffle-asparagus pairing is traditional in southern France, but truffle and leek create an equally convincing blend. The truffle and olive oil sauce offsets the crunchiness of the main ingredients.

•Jean-Louis Nomicos•
Cooked and Raw Green Asparagus Tips with Warm Oysters and Winkles

Jean-Louis Nomicos relishes the bitterness of very thinly sliced raw asparagus. In this recipe the flavor of cooked asparagus is intensified by the distinctive grassy tang of the raw vegetable. This in turn brings out the sea-water taste of the oyster juices, lightened by the presence of the winkles. But the dish's most interesting feature is the textural contrast between melt-in-the-mouth oysters and crunchy asparagus and winkles.

•Sylvain Portay•
Roast Asparagus Parmesan, with Steamed Morels au naturel and Poached Egg

The subtle bitterness of cooked asparagus is a marvelous match for the smoky flavor of morels. Here, all the ingredients are left as "natural" as possible: the *bourgeoise* asparagus is sautéed in unsalted butter and seasoned only with Parmesan cheese, the morels are simply steamed with a little garlic and scallions (virtually essential with mushrooms), and the egg poached. The asparagus and morel sauce, enhanced by a dash of lemon juice, adds the perfect finishing touch.

•Jean-François Piège•
Charcoal-grilled Villelaure Asparagus, Egg Polignac and Truffle Essence

This dish uses green *bourgeoise* asparagus which are large and fleshy enough to stand being both sautéed and char-grilled. In Provence, the first asparagus usually appear in time for their traditional marriage with the last truffles of the season. Together they serve to highlight the perfectly-cooked egg. The *foie gras* adds a final, opulent touch.

•Alessandro Stratta•
Glazed Asparagus and Veal Sweetbreads Fricassée with Sherry Vinegar

The asparagus are cooked in a skillet to preserve maximum flavor. Their delicate, bitter, grassy notes provide a counterpoint to the sweetish, nutty taste of the fried sweetbreads. The crispness of the asparagus and the tenderness of the sweetbreads also create a contrast of textures. Sherry vinegar adds a touch of acidity to the sauce, which is reinforced by the salad seasoning. Chives and chervil highlight the fresh flavor of the asparagus.

Early Purple Asparagus, Spring Leeks and Late-Season Black Truffles

BY FRANCK CERUTTI

Peel the asparagus and cut all the spears to the same size. Cut off the roots of the leeks. Simply trim the ends of the green parts.

Bring 3 ½ cups (80 cl) of chicken stock to a boil in a saucepan. Add the leeks and cook in the boiling stock for 20 minutes.

Bring a saucepan of salted water to a boil. Gently place the asparagus in the water, return to a boil and cook for 4-5 minutes. Drain the asparagus and leeks.

Pare the truffle to make it a regular shape. Crush the parings with a fork. Cut 8 slices from the truffle and reserve the rest.

Arrange the asparagus in a skillet. Fold the leeks to the same size as the asparagus spears and add them to the skillet. Add the crushed truffle parings, the 8 slices of truffle, olive oil, butter and ½ cup chicken stock. Season with salt. Bring to a boil over a low heat, moving the skillet round in a clockwise direction.

The emulsion produced is very delicate: if the fat separates from the stock, this means there is too much oil and butter, in which case add a little more stock. Speed is essential if this dish is to succeed. It should take no longer than 5 minutes.

To round off the wonderful olive oil sauce, add a trickle each of balsamic vinegar and sherry vinegar to sharpen it. Adjust the seasoning.

Serve immediately, seasoned with the rest of the raw truffle, grated, and a sprinkling of fine salt.

4 SERVINGS

- 20 plump purple asparagus from the Nice region
- 20 slender spring leeks
- 1 quart (1 l) light chicken stock (see page 130)
- 1 black truffle weighing 1 ½ ounces (40 g)
- ¼ cup (5 cl) olive oil
- 1 ½ level tablespoons (20 g) unsalted butter
- Balsamic vinegar
- Sherry vinegar
- Fine salt
- Table salt
- Freshly ground pepper

Wine suggestion: a Provençal white, such as Bandol cuvée spéciale, Domaine Tempier, E.A.R.L. Peyraud.

Cooked and Raw Green Asparagus Tips with Warm Oysters and Winkles

BY JEAN-LOUIS NOMICOS

Soak the winkles for 2 hours in cold water, with plenty of coarse salt. Bring a saucepan of water – sea water, if possible – to a boil. Add 2 pinches of Cayenne pepper. Rinse the winkles then place them in the boiling water and cook for between 5 and 8 minutes, according to size. Drain and remove from the shells with a toothpick.

Peel the asparagus and trim them to a length of 3 inches (7 cm). Slice the trimmed-off bases diagonally into chunks and place them in a saucepan with 1 ½ tablespoons (20 g) butter. Soften them over a low heat for 5 minutes. Season with salt and pepper. Cover with chicken stock. Bring to a boil and cook for 15 minutes. To cool the asparagus, stand the saucepan on a bed of ice. Stir and pass through a chinois (or fine sieve).

Open the oysters. Reserve the 12 best ones and their liquor. Coarsely chop the 3 remaining oysters, reserving the liquor.

Cut 6 asparagus tips lengthwise into thin slices, using a Japanese mandolin.

Heat 2 ¼ tablespoons (30 g) butter in a skillet. Add the asparagus tips and season with salt and pepper. Cook over a medium heat adding a little chicken stock from time to time and shaking the skillet.

When the asparagus tips are still slightly crisp and well-coated with butter, add the 12 oysters, winkles, sliced asparagus and half the oyster liquor, and gently warm through.

Add 1 level tablespoon (10 g) butter to the asparagus purée, then whisk. Add the coarsely chopped oysters and their liquor. Add the whipped cream and a drop of lemon juice to create an emulsion. Season lightly with a pinch of Cayenne pepper.

Arrange 3 oysters, 7 asparagus tips, winkles and sliced raw asparagus attractively on each plate, surrounded by asparagus purée.

4 SERVINGS

- 14 ounces (400 g) winkles
- 15 Gilardeau n°3 oysters
- 34 green asparagus
- Cayenne pepper
- 5 tablespoons (60 g) unsalted butter
- 1 cup (25 cl) light chicken stock (see page 130)
- 1 tablespoon whipped cream
- Lemon juice
- Coarse salt
- Fine salt, freshly ground pepper

SPECIAL UTENSILS

- 1 Japanese mandolin

Wine suggestion: a dry, flinty white Val de Loire, such as Vouvray, Domaine de la Fontainerie, C. Dhoye-Deruet, 1996.

Charcoal-grilled Villelaure Asparagus, Egg Polignac and Truffle Essence

BY JEAN-FRANÇOIS PIÈGE

The truffles and eggs may, if necessary, be kept in a jar for 2 days prior to use.

Prepare the Périgueux sauce: peel and slice the scallions. Crush the garlic cloves. Fry the veal in a cast-iron stew pot with a little oil. Add the butter and continue to fry the meat until lightly caramelized. Add the scallions and garlic. Leave to soften over a low heat for a few minutes then skim off the fat. Moisten with the Madeira, scraping the base of the pot with a spatula. Cook until all the liquid has evaporated. Add the veal stock and the thyme, and cook until all the liquid has evaporated. Add the veal *jus* and reduce to a syrupy consistency. Pass through a chinois (or fine sieve) and check the seasoning. Add a little freshly ground pepper and the minced truffle.

Peel and wash the asparagus. Reserve 2 spears. Place the rest in a skillet with a little olive oil. Cover and simmer gently for 5 minutes. Add just enough water to cover and simmer gently for 10 minutes.

Scrub the truffles under running water, then dry them and pare them into a regular shape. Reserve one truffle and cut the rest into fairly thick slices.

Peel the green onion and cut into a fine julienne. Soften the sliced truffles over a low heat with 2 tablespoons (30 g) foaming butter. Add the green onion and cook until soft. Add the Madeira, scraping the base of the pan with a spatula. Reduce the Madeira by half, then add the truffle jus and chicken stock. Simmer over a low heat for 10 minutes. Bind with 2 table-spoons (30 g) butter. Season with truffle essence (see below) and freshly ground pepper.

Preheat the oven to 350°F (180°C; gas mark 4). Break one egg into each ramekin, making sure the yolk is well centered. Place the ramekins in a *bain-marie* and bake in the oven for 5-8 minutes: the yolks should be hot and the whites set. Turn out carefully onto the plates.

Cut the asparagus spears in half lengthwise from top to bottom. Coat with olive oil and grill over charcoal for 1-2 minutes on each side, turning the asparagus halfway so that they are streaked with color from the grill. A griddle may be used instead of a charcoal grill. Cut the raw asparagus into slivers.

Cut the baguette in half lengthwise and toast on one side. Using a teaspoon, take fine slivers of *foie gras* from the jar and arrange them neatly on the bread.

Arrange the cooked truffles and grilled asparagus on each plate with the baguette (or present the bread separately). Sprinkle with raw asparagus slivers. Pour a little Périgueux sauce alongside and serve the rest in a small earthenware dish. Grate the raw truffle over each plate.

Use the truffle parings to make truffle essence. Place the parings in a saucepan, add enough chicken stock to cover and leave to infuse, uncovered, over a very low heat for 30 minutes. Pass through a chinois (or fine sieve), and keep the essence in an airtight jar.

2 SERVINGS

- 4 ounces (100 g) black Richerenches truffles
- 2 new-laid eggs
- 14 large, green, "bourgeoise" asparagus
- 1 green onion
- 6 tablespoons (10 cl) olive oil
- Light chicken stock (see page 130)
- 5 tablespoons (60 g) unsalted butter
- 2 tablespoons Madeira
- 6 tablespoons (10 cl) truffle jus
- 1 scant cup (20 cl) chicken stock
- 2 tablespoons truffle essence
- 1 farmhouse baguette
- 2 ounces (50 g) preserved *foie gras*
- Freshly ground pepper

PÉRIGUEUX SAUCE

- 14 ounces (400 g) breast or loin of veal, cut into pieces
- 2 ounces (50 g) scallions, 2 garlic cloves
- Grapeseed oil
- 2 tablespoons (30 g) unsalted butter, 6 tablespoons (10 cl) Madeira
- 1 sprig thyme
- 2 cups (50 cl) veal stock (adapted from chicken stock recipe, page 130)
- 2 cups (50 cl) veal jus (see page 130)
- 2 ounces (50 g) minced truffle

Wine suggestion: a white wine from the Rhône Valley, such as Condrieu "La Doriane", M. Guigal, 1994.

Roast Asparagus Parmesan, with Steamed Morels au naturel and Poached Egg

BY SYLVAIN PORTAY

Peel the asparagus. Tie them in a bundle. Bring a large saucepan of water to a boil and add salt. Place the asparagus in the boiling water for about 15 minutes until cooked but still slightly firm. Drain immediately, refresh in iced water, then drain and untie.

Cook the 6 asparagus tips in boiling salted water for 10 minutes. Refresh in iced water and drain. Rub the asparagus tips through a sieve and pour the resulting purée in a small skillet. Place the skillet over a very low flame to reduce, stirring constantly. Leave to cool.

Remove the morel stalks, then sort and wash them very carefully to remove any grit. Cut the larger ones in half lengthwise. Drain the morels.
Peel, degerm and mince the garlic. Peel and finely mince the scallion.

Heat a little olive oil in a small saucepan. Add the morels, garlic and scallion, then cover and cook for a few minutes over a medium heat. When the mushrooms begin to sweat, add 1 ½ tablespoons (20 g) butter and continue to cook, covered, for 10 minutes over a low heat.

Bring a wide saucepan of water to a boil and add 2 tablespoons vinegar. Break an egg into a cup. Bring the cup as close as possible to the surface of the water and tip the egg into the pan in a single movement. Using a slotted spoon, cover the yolk with the white. Repeat the same process for each egg and cook for 3 minutes, without allowing the water to boil. Remove the eggs from the pan with the slotted spoon, in the same order as you placed them in the water. Drain them on a clean cloth.

While the eggs are cooking, melt 5 tablespoons (60 g) butter in a skillet and brown the asparagus lightly and evenly. Sprinkle with Parmesan cheese, rolling the spears in the grated cheese, and remove from the heat.

Bring the morels and their liquid to a boil. Add a tablespoon of asparagus purée, bind with 1 ½ tablespoons (20 g) butter, adjust the seasoning and add a squeeze of lemon juice.

Arrange 3 asparagus spears in a fan shape on each plate. Cover with 1 tablespoon of morels. Place the poached egg on top, coat generously with sauce and garnish with a few morels. Sprinkle with chervil leaves and serve immediately.

4 SERVINGS

- 12 large green asparagus spears
- 6 asparagus tips
- 5 ounces (150 g) morels
- 1 garlic clove
- 1 scallion
- Olive oil
- 1 stick (100 g) unsalted butter
- 2 tablespoons vinegar
- 4 eggs
- Scant ½ cup (40 g) grated Parmesan cheese
- Lemon juice
- Chervil leaves
- Salt
- Freshly ground pepper

Wine suggestion: a white Burgundy, such as Chablis grand cru "Valmur", François & Jean-Marie Raveneau, 1990.

Glazed Asparagus and Veal Sweetbreads Fricassée with Sherry Vinegar

BY ALESSANDRO STRATTA

Leave the sweetbreads packed in ice overnight to remove the blood.

Peel the asparagus and trim the spears to the same length. Plunge them into a saucepan of boiling salted water for 1 minute. Drain and place on a clean cloth.

Heat a little olive oil in a skillet and add 3 ½ tablespoons (40 g) butter. Place the asparagus in the hot fat and roll them around so that they color evenly. Season with salt and cook for 15 minutes. Add the chicken stock and shake the pan to coat the asparagus. Sprinkle with chives.

Drain the sweetbreads and dry them carefully. Cut into ½-inch (1-cm) dice. Season with salt and pepper. Coat generously with flour and shake to remove the excess.

Peel, degerm and mince the garlic cloves. Peel and mince the scallions.

Heat 1 tablespoon olive oil in a skillet. Add 3 ½ tablespoons (40 g) butter and the sweetbreads. Brown over a high heat for 1 minutes, then add the garlic and scallions. Sauté for 30-45 seconds. Add 2 tablespoons sherry vinegar, scraping the base of the pan with a spatula. Allow all the vinegar to evaporate, then add the veal *jus* and reduce to a syrupy consistence. Sprinkle with parsley and check the seasoning.

Prepare the garnish: wash and dry the lamb's lettuce and curly endive heart. Place the salad leaves in a bowl with the chopped chives. Mix the sherry vinegar with salt and stir in the oil. Toss the salad in the vinaigrette dressing. Wash and dry the radish and cut into slivers.

Arrange the dressed salad in the center of each plate, topped with asparagus and finally the sweetbreads. Garnish with the slivers of radish and chervil leaves.

4 SERVINGS

- 1 generous pound (500 g) veal sweetbreads
- 20 "bourgeoise" asparagus spears
- 2 tablespoons olive oil
- 7 tablespoons (80 g) unsalted butter
- 4 tablespoons chicken stock
- 2 tablespoons minced chives
- 3 tablespoons flour
- 2 garlic cloves
- 2 scallions
- 2 tablespoons sherry vinegar
- 4 tablespoons veal jus (see page 130)
- 4 tablespoons flat-leaf parsley, coarsely chopped
- Salt, freshly ground pepper

GARNISH

- 2 ounces (50 g) lamb's lettuce
- 1 white curly endive heart
- 1 tablespoon minced chives
- 1 tablespoon sherry vinegar
- 2 tablespoons olive oil
- 1 large red radish
- 4 sprigs chervil

Wine suggestion: a white Alsace wine, such as Muscat grand cru "Golddert", Domaine Zind-Humbrecht.

Semi-dried Pasta with Cream Sauce, Truffles, and Ragout of Cockscombs and Chicken Kidney

BY ALAIN DUCASSE

This dish is mentioned by the Michelin Guide as a specialty of my Paris restaurant. It juxtaposes different taste experiences: the delicacy of the pasta and cream, the strong flavor of the cockscombs and chicken kidney, all enhanced by the fragrance of black truffle. Here, two different culinary cultures come face to face: the Italian, symbolized by pasta, and the French, with its characteristic richness and technical skill.

4 SERVINGS

FROM THE MARKET
- **½ ounce (10 g) minced black truffle**
- **12 ounces (400 g) Breton lobster (one generous slice and one claw per person)**
- **1 tablespoon (10 g) unsalted butter**
- **Olive oil**

Prepare the veal *jus*: heat the oil or chicken fat in a cast iron pot. Fry the veal in the fat. When the meat is well colored and begins to adhere to the pot, discard the fat and add the butter, scraping the base of the pot with a spatula to remove any sediment. Cover with water and allow all the liquid to evaporate. Half cover with more water and cook until evaporated. Add enough water to cover the meat and simmer for 2 hours over a very low heat. Strain through a chinois (or fine sieve) and refrigerate. The butter will harden to form a protective layer on top.

Prepare the chicken stock: place the chicken carcasses in a large stew pot, cover with cold water and bring to a boil over a high heat. Boil for 5 minutes, then rinse the carcasses in cold water and clean the pot. Replace the carcasses in the pot, add the coarsely chopped vegetables, parsley, coarse salt and peppercorns. Cover with cold water. Simmer for 1 ½-2 hours over a low heat, skimming from time to time, then strain the stock. Keep it in the refrigerator for a maximum of 24 hours. Any stock not required should be frozen immediately.

Make the semi-dried pasta: heap the flour onto the work surface, break the eggs into the center and work them into the flour. Knead by hand to create an even dough, then encase in saran wrap and leave to rest in the refrigerator for 2 hours.

Roll out the dough as thinly as possible on a lightly floured work surface. Cut into rounds with a 4-inch (95-mm) cookie cutter. Roll each round into an oval shape with a rolling pin. Roll the ovals around a wooden pastry rod, leaving a little "tongue" protruding. Press the pasta rolls gently to seal them, leaving one end protruding (to make them easy to pick up), and leave to dry for several hours.

Start preparing the ragout: place the cockscombs and kidneys in two separate saucepans of cold water and bring to a boil. As soon as the water boils, drain and refresh in iced water.

Leave the kidneys whole, but remove the skins and cores. Pour 2 ½ cups (60 cl) chicken stock into a saucepan and add the kidneys. Simmer gently for 10 minutes, then drain and leave to cool.

Remove the membranes from the cockscombs and cut the crests and bases into pieces. Pour 2 ½ cups (60 cl) chicken stock into another saucepan, bring to a boil, add the cockscombs and simmer over a low heat for 1 hour. Drain and leave to cool.

Place the sweetbreads in a saucepan of cold water, add salt, bring slowly to a boil, then drain and refresh the sweetbreads under cold running water. Preheat the oven to 300°F (150°C; gas mark 2).

Cut the carrot, onion, celery and scallion into small dice. Melt 3 tablespoons (40 g) unsalted butter in a small ovenproof skillet, add the vegetables, then cover and soften for 5 minutes. Lay the sweetbreads on top of the vegetables, add ½ cup chicken stock, cover and bake in the oven for 30 minutes, without allowing the sweetbreads to take color. When they are cooked, divide them carefully into 12 *noisettes*, about ¾ ounce (20 g) each. Strain and reserve the cooking juices.

Prepare the cream sauce for the pasta: place 1 ½ tablespoons (20 g) unsalted butter in a saucepan, stir in the flour, then simmer the roux over

Veal jus
- 4 ½ pounds (2 kg) breast or rib of veal, cut into pieces
- Generous ½ cup (15 cl) olive oil or 10 tablespoons (150 g) chicken fat
- 10 tablespoons (150 g) unsalted butter

Light chicken stock
- 6 ½ pounds (3 kg) chicken carcasses
- 6 ounces (150 g) onions, peeled
- 3 scallions, peeled
- 7 ounces (200 g) carrots, peeled
- 6 ounces (150 g) celery ribs
- 4 ounces (100 g) leeks, green portions only
- 1 tomato
- 5 parsley stems
- 1 tablespoon coarse salt
- 1 tablespoon black peppercorns

Semi-dried pasta
- 2 ⅔ cups (400 g) durum wheat flour
- 4 medium eggs

● Cut the dough into rounds using a 4-inch (95-mm) cookie cutter.

● Roll the rounds of dough into ovals.

● Roll the dough around wooden pastry rods, leaving a small tongue protruding.

● Place the kidneys and cockscombs in separate saucepans of cold water and bring to a boil.

● Remove the membrane covering the cockscombs and cut the crests and bases into pieces.

● Braise the sweetbreads and chopped vegetables in chicken stock for 30 minutes in the oven.

● Carefully cut the sweetbreads into *noisettes* ¾ ounce (20 g) each.

● Prepare a roux. Whisk the mixture while adding the milk. Cook the *béchamel* for 5 minutes.

Cockscomb and chicken kidney ragout

- **12 cockscombs**
- **12 chicken's kidneys**
- **12 ounces (360 g) veal sweetbreads**
- **½ carrot**
- **¼ onion**
- **4 inches (10 cm) celery**
- **¼ scallion**
- **6 tablespoons (80 g) butter**
- **2 ounces (50 g) black truffle**
- **4 ¼ ounces (120 g) chanterelles**
- **Lemon juice**
- **Sea salt**
- **Freshly ground pepper**

a very low heat for 3-4 minutes. Leave until completely cold. Bring the milk to a boil, then pour the boiling milk over the roux, stirring with a balloon whisk. Cook the *béchamel,* which will form the basis for the cream sauce, for 5 minutes. Stir in the cream and mascarpone, remove from the heat and add 2 tablespoons (4 cl) of the truffle juice and the grated Beaufort cheese. Season lightly with salt.

While preparing the sauce, bring 2 cups (50 cl) chicken stock to a boil. Pick up the pasta rolls up by the protruding tongue, place 20 rolls in the boiling stock, return to a boil and cook for 10 minutes. Drain the pasta, add to the cream sauce and simmer for a further 2 minutes.

Heat ½ cup (10 cl) veal *jus* very gently in a saucepan, without allowing it to boil. Add 1 tablespoon (2 cl) truffle juice and ½ ounce (10 g) minced black truffle. Remove the pan from the heat, cover and leave to infuse.

● Whisk the heavy cream and mascarpone into the *béchamel.*

● Stir 2 tablespoons (4 cl) truffle *jus* into the cream sauce. Remove from the heat.

● Drain the pasta as soon as it is cooked, then add it to the cream sauce.

● Heat ½ cup (10 cl) veal *jus* and add the minced truffle and 1 tablespoon (2 cl) truffle *jus.*

Finish the ragout: cut 2 ounces (50 g) black truffle into slices. Clean the chanterelle stalks, then quickly wash the mushrooms and dry them with a cloth. Melt 1 ½ tablespoons (20 g) unsalted butter in a skillet and sauté the chanterelles for a few minutes until all the juices have evaporated. Season with salt.

Place the cockscombs, kidneys, sweetbread *noisettes*, chanterelles, truffle and the cooking juices from the sweetbread in a skillet over a very low heat and stir to bind the mixture. Add 1 ½ tablespoons (20 g) butter, cut into small pieces, moving the skillet round and round to bind. Adjust the seasoning with sea salt, freshly ground pepper and a few drops of lemon juice.

Heat a little olive oil in a skillet and add 1 level tablespoon (10 g) butter. Seal the lobster slices and claws in the hot oil and butter over a high heat, then arrange on top of the ragout and keep hot.

Carefully arrange five pieces of pasta on each plate. Lay first the cockscomb and kidney ragout and then the lobster on top. Surround with the rest of the cream sauce and veal *jus* with minced truffle. Serve piping hot.

Cream sauce

- 1 ½ tablespoons (20 g) unsalted butter
- Scant ¼ cup (20 g) flour
- ¾ cup (20 cl) milk
- 3 tablespoons (40 g) Echiré cream (top quality heavy cream)
- 3 tablespoons (40 g) mascarpone
- 4 tablespoons truffle jus
- ¾ cup (60 g) grated Beaufort cheese
- Sea salt

Special utensils

- 1 cookie cutter, 4 inches (95 mm) in diameter
- Wooden pastry rods, ½ inch (10 mm) in diameter

Wine suggestion: a white Bordeaux from the Graves region, such as Pessac-Léognan blanc, Les Planties de Haut-Brion, 1994.

● Sauté the chanterelles in butter until all the liquid has evaporated.

● Bind the cockscombs, kidneys, sweetbreads and chanterelles with the pan juices from the sweetbreads.

● Seal the lobster pieces over a high heat in olive oil and butter.

● Arrange the pasta on four plates with the ragout on top. Pour over the truffle-flavored veal *jus.*

" WHATEVER THE VARIETY, A GRAIN OF WHEAT CONSISTS OF SEVERAL PARTS OF DIFFERING NUTRITIONAL VALUE: THE OUTER HUSK, REMOVED STRAIGHT AFTER HARVESTING, AND THE GRAIN, WHICH IS COMPOSED OF THREE PARTS: THE BRAN COAT AROUND THE KERNEL, THE KERNEL OR ENDOSPERM AND THE EMBRYO OR GERM. "

CONTENTS

● Alain Ducasse ●
Semi-dried Pasta with Cream Sauce, Truffles, and Ragout of Cockscombs and Chicken Kidney

Alain Ducasse was inspired to create this recipe after reading Lucien Tendet's classic book *La Table au pays de Brillat-Savarin*. The idea of combining the culinary styles of France and Italy appealed to him. The garnish provides an interplay between various different textures and the pasta, too, takes an unusual shape. The distinctive flavors of the truffles, cockscombs and kidneys, and cheese, contrast with the sweetness and subtlety of the cream sauce, sweetbreads and pasta.

● Franck Cerutti ●
Spelt Soup with Ewe's Milk Curd Cheese and Mature Pecorino

This recipe brings back memories of childhood, with cheese in the soup, and history lessons which told of how Roman legions were fed on spelt. Here, a traditional Provençal soup is given the *grande cuisine* treatment, with the garnish prepared separately to highlight the distinctive flavors of the ingredients. Cheese appears in two guises, fresh ewe's milk curd cheese and mature Pecorino. The first, traditional to the Nice region, adds freshness and thickness to the soup; the second, an Italian specialty, is used as a seasoning.

• Jean-Louis Nomicos •
Golden Galette with Cooked and Raw Black Truffles and Celery Root with Périgueux Sauce

Like everyone who has worked alongside Alain Ducasse, Jean-Louis Nomicos likes to cook with traditional vegetables, but, as this recipe proves, is just as enthusiastic about pasta and gnocchi. Raw and cooked truffles, offering contrasts of both texture and taste, are combined with celery root. The Périgueux sauce fulfills its classic role of adding richness and enhancing the overall flavor.

• Sylvain Portay •
Champagne-grape Marmalade Tartlets with Crisp Puffed Wheat Cookies and Wheat Nougatine

Sylvain Portay uses wheat in all its guises: flour for making the tartlet pastry, as well as two types of wheat grains. By preparing wheat products in different ways he brings together distinctive textures and sweet and bitter-sweet flavors. Whipped cream provides a luscious counterpoint to the nougatine; the dense marmalade is sandwiched between the feather-light cookie and the more solid tartlet crust.

• Jean-François Piège •
Upside-down Wild Strawberry Tart

The idea of this dish was to place wheat center stage, to make the pastry "a must" and the upside-down tart simply irresistible. The problem was to make the filling visible, and Jean-François Piège came up with the notion of creating a "window" of palest caramel. It is a dish requiring considerable technical skill, but wheat is such a mundane ingredient that it was necessary to give it a little more glamour. Sorbet and freshly-made yogurt add the milky flavor that so perfectly complements strawberries.

• Alessandro Stratta •
Mascarpone Ravioli with Spinach, Chanterelles and Parmesan Cheese

Alessandro Stratta treats wheat in a highly traditional way to prepare ravioli with a slightly elastic texture. Cut open, the raviolis reveal the richness of the mascarpone which provides a "neutral" taste to temper the strong taste of garlic. The spinach adds a slightly bitter-sweet flavor, while the shavings of Parmesan provide both seasoning for the whole dish and a firm texture to contrast with the softness of the chanterelles.

Spelt Soup with Ewe's Milk Curd Cheese and Mature Pecorino

BY FRANCK CERUTTI

Soak the spelt overnight in a bowl of cold water.

Bone the chicken leg and cut into four pieces. Cut the streaky salt belly pork into large dice. Peel and slice the onion half. Peel the garlic clove, cut it in half and degerm. Peel and quarter the tomato.

Heat a little olive oil in a cast iron stew pot. Fry the chicken and salt belly pork in the hot oil over a medium heat for about 10 minutes until lightly colored.

Add the onion and garlic, cover and soften over a low heat for 5 minutes. Add the tomato quarters and sage leaves. Season with salt.

Add the saffron threads and stir carefully. Drain the spelt. Reserve 2 ounces (50 g) for the garnish. Add the spelt and 1 quart (1 l) chicken stock to the pot. Cover, bring to a boil and simmer gently for 1 hour.

After 1 hour, stir the soup and adjust the seasoning. If the soup is too thick, add a little chicken stock or hot milk.

Prepare the garnish: peel the carrot and scallions. Clean the mushrooms. Cut the vegetables into ⅛-inch (2.5 mm) dice. Remove any tough strings from the celery and cut into dice the same size. Soften the diced vegetables in 1 ½ tablespoons (20 g) butter over a low heat. Bring a saucepan of water to a boil, add the 2 ounces (50 g) of reserved spelt and cook for 15 minutes. Mix the spelt and vegetables with the chicken *jus* and add seasoning.

Whip the cream lightly until it just begins to peak. Grate the Pecorino (ewe's milk cheese from Tuscany or Sardinia which can be grated like Parmesan).

Divide the soup between four plates. Place the curd cheese in the center of each plate of soup, using a round cookie cutter as a template. Season the curd cheese with a few grains of fine salt. Arrange the garnish on top. Drizzle with a little olive oil and a few drops of balsamic vinegar. Add 1 tablespoon of lightly whipped cream. Serve the Pecorino separately.

4 SERVINGS

- 1 ¼ cups (300 g) fine spelt (from a healthfood shop)
- 1 chicken leg
- 3 ounces (80 g) salt belly pork
- ½ white onion, 1 garlic clove
- 1 ripe tomato
- ¼ cup (5 cl) olive oil
- 4 sage leaves
- 1 pinch saffron threads
- 1 quart (1 l) light chicken stock (see page 130)
- 4 tablespoons cream, well chilled
- 4 ounces (100 g) hard ewe's milk cheese or Sardinian Pecorino
- 7-ounce (200 g) carton ewe's milk curd cheese (such as Basque Mamia or fresh Brousse from Nice)
- 1 teaspoon balsamic vinegar
- Fine salt
- Salt, freshly milled pepper

GARNISH

- 1 carrot, 2 scallions
- 1 cep or 3 cultivated mushroom caps
- 2 sticks celery (or equivalent quantity of celery root)
- 1 ½ tablespoons (20 g) unsalted butter
- 1 tablespoon chicken jus

Wine suggestion: a white wine from Camporosso, Italy, such as Vermentino from M. Romagnoli's Giuncheo estate.

Golden Galette with Cooked and Raw Black Truffles and Celery Root with Périgueux Sauce

BY JEAN-LOUIS NOMICOS

Peel the truffles while retaining their shape. Reserve the parings for the sauce.

Prepare the Périgueux sauce: peel and slice the scallions. Brown the beef in a saucepan over a medium heat. Add three-quarters of the scallions and the *mignonette* (coarsely ground white) pepper. Soften the scallions for 5 minutes. Add half the port, scraping the base of the pan with a spatula. Reduce the pan juices by three-quarters. Add the beef *jus.* Reduce until the liquid becomes syrupy, skimming regularly. Strain through a chinois (or fine sieve).

Place 1 ½ tablespoons (20 g) butter in a saucepan with the truffle shavings. Soften over a low heat, mashing the truffle with a fork. Add the rest of the scallions, the remaining port and the truffle *jus.* Cook until almost all the liquid has evaporated, then add the beef jus. Stir the remaining 2 ¼ tablespoons butter (30 g), a small knob at a time. Check the seasoning and keep the sauce hot.

Preheat the oven to 400°F (200°C; gas mark 6). Cut the celery root into very thin slices, no more than ⅛ inch (2 mm) thick. Using a 1 ½-inch (4-cm) cookie cutter, cut 16 rounds of celery root per serving. Place the rounds in a salad bowl and season with salt and pepper. Add the potato flour and mix carefully. Drizzle with 4 tablespoons warm, clarified butter. Arrange the rounds of celery root in overlapping circles in 4 nonstick baking tins, 4-inches (10 cm) in diameter. Bake in the oven for 10 minutes, then turn out onto a cooling rack.

Arrange the rounds of puff pastry, 3 inches (7 cm) in diameter and ⅛ inch (3 mm) thick, on a nonstick baking sheet. Mix 1 teaspoon water with the egg yolk. Brush the pastry with this glaze, taking care it does not run down the sides. Make a light criss-cross pattern on the top with the point of a knife. Bake in the oven for 7 minutes at 375°F (190°C; gas mark 5).

Cut half the truffles into thin slices, no more than ⅛ inch (2 mm) thick. Soften gently in a skillet with 1 ½ tablespoons (20 g) butter. Season with salt and pepper and add the scallion. Add the sherry and port, scraping the base of the pan with a spatula. Add the truffle *jus* and chicken stock. Stir in the cream and cook for 2 minutes. Remove from the heat, cover and leave to infuse.

Slice the top off the pastry rounds and remove the layers of uncooked pastry underneath. Place a pastry round in the center of each plate. Arrange 5 slices of cooked truffle around the edge of the pastry and place the rest under the pastry, without adding sauce. Thinly slice the raw truffles and arrange them in an overlapping circle with a little sauce in the middle. Arrange the hot celery root galettes on top of the raw truffles. Cover the cooked truffles in truffle sauce. Spoon a little Périgueux sauce onto the plates. Place the pastry "lid" on top of the truffle so that the filling is visible. Pour a little warm clarified butter over the pastry to give it a glossy finish.

4 SERVINGS

- 4 rounds puff pastry (see page 92)
- 5 ½ ounces (160 g) black truffles
- 1 celery root
- 1 teaspoon (5 g) potato flour
- 5 tablespoons (60 g) clarified unsalted butter (see page 171)
- 1 egg yolk, 1 ½ tablespoons (20 g) unsalted butter
- 1 teaspoon (5 g) finely minced scallion
- 1 tablespoon Tio Pepe sherry
- 1 tablespoon red port
- 3 tablespoons truffle jus
- 4 tablespoons light chicken stock (see page 130)
- 3 tablespoons light cream
- Salt, freshly ground pepper

PÉRIGUEUX SAUCE

- 2 scallions
- 5 ounces (150 g) lean short plate of beef, cut into chunks
- ½ teaspoon mignonette (coarsely ground white) pepper
- ⅓ cup (8 cl) red port
- ½ cup (10 cl) beef jus (see page 112)
- 2 ounces (50 g) unsalted butter
- 3 tablespoons truffle jus

SPECIAL UTENSILS

- 1 cookie cutter, 1 ½ inches (4-cm) in diameter
- 4 nonstick baking tins, 4 inches (10 cm) in diameter

Wine suggestion: a red wine from Provence, such as Coteaux d'Aix "les Baux", Domaine de Trévaillon, 1986.

Upside-down Wild Strawberry Tart

BY JEAN-FRANÇOIS PIÈGE

Prepare the tartlets: roll the dough as thinly as possible, sprinkling it with confectioners' sugar. Cut it into strips 1 ½ inches (3 cm) wide and 9 inches (24 cm) long. Arrange the strips on a nonstick baking sheet. Leave to dry in the open air for 6 hours.

Preheat the oven to 350°F (180°C; gas mark 4). Place the baking sheet in the oven and cook for 12-15 minutes, in order to caramelize the sugar in the dough. As soon as the pastry is cooked, roll the strips around 4 vacherin rings, 3 inches (7 cm) in diameter. Leave to cool then remove the rings.

Place the sugar lumps in a saucepan with 2 tablespoons water. Melt the sugar over a low heat, then bring to a boil and cook to obtain a very pale caramel. Turn the caramel out onto baking parchment and immediately spread it with a spatula. Using a 3-inch (7 cm) cookie cutter, cut the caramel into circles.

Prepare the condensed milk sorbet: bring the fresh milk to a boil. Leave to cool completely and then dissolve the skimmed milk powder in the fresh milk. Add the sugar and condensed milk, ensuring that both dissolve completely. Strain through a chinois (or fine sieve), transfer to an ice cream maker and freeze.

Prepare the wild strawberry yogurt: preheat the oven to its very lowest setting. Whisk the egg yolks and sugar in a salad bowl until they turn white. Add the fresh milk and crème fraîche. Pour the mixture into an earthenware dish and cook in the oven for about 3 hours. Leave to cool.

When the yogurt is cold, remove the skin from the surface. Gently break up the yogurt with a fork. Add the strawberries and stir them into the yogurt, taking great care not to damage them.

Prepare the strawberry *jus*: wash, hull and dry the strawberries, and place them in a salad bowl with the sugar. Stir, then cover the bowl with saran wrap and leave to marinate in the refrigerator for 6 hours.

Assemble the tartlets: strain the strawberry juice through a piece of muslin or gauze. Cover the 11 ounces (300 g) of strawberries with the juice. Place a pastry circle on each plate and fill with strawberry yogurt. Arrange the juice-covered strawberries on top. To finish, close each tartlet with a round of caramelized sugar, so that they look like upside-down tartlets, with the filling visible through the transparent caramel.

Pour a little strawberry *jus* onto each plate beside the tartlet, and on top place a portion of sorbet, molded into an oval shape with a tablespoon.

4 SERVINGS

- 12 ounces (350 g) puff pastry
  (see page 92)
- 1 cup (100 g) confectioners'
  sugar
- 7 ounces (200 g) lump sugar
- 11 ounces (300 g) wild
  strawberries

CONDENSED MILK SORBET
- 4 cups fresh, full cream milk
- 2 ⅓ cups (210 g) powdered
  skimmed milk
- 2 ¼ cups (650 g) condensed milk
- 2 ½ cups (245 g) sugar

WILD STRAWBERRY YOGURT
- 8 egg yolks
- ¼ cup (100 g) sugar
- 1 cup plus 1 tablespoon fresh,
  full cream milk
- 1 cup plus 1 tablespoon light
  crème fraîche
- 11 ounces (300 g)
  wild strawberries

STRAWBERRY JUS
- 2 pounds (1 kg) wild strawberries
- ¾ cup (170 g) sugar

SPECIAL UTENSILS
- vacherin rings, 3 inches (7 cm)
  in diameter
- 1 cookie cutter, 3 inches (7 cm)
  in diameter

*Wine suggestion: a naturally
sweet white wine, such as
Rivesaltes, Mas Christines, 1994.*

Champagne-grape Marmalade Tartlets with Crisp Puffed Wheat Cookies and Wheat Nougatine

BY SYLVAIN PORTAY

Prepare the sweet shortcrust pastry: place the softened butter in a blender and process until soft and smooth. Add the confectioners' sugar and blend to obtain a creamy mixture. Add the flour and salt, followed by the whole egg and the egg yolk. When the dough is even, wrap it in saran wrap and leave to rest in the refrigerator for at least 1 hour.

Make the grape marmalade: wash and dry the grapes, deseed, then place the grapes in a skillet. Mash with a fork and bring to a boil over a high heat. Add the red wine and simmer over a low heat for 20 minutes to obtain a compote. Strain the marmalade through a sieve and reserve the juice separately. Refrigerate the juice and marmalade.

Prepare the wheat nougatine: preheat the oven to 425°F (220°C; gas mark 7). Place the glucose, sugar, butter, milk and pectin in a copper pan. Whisk and cook over a high heat until the mixture reaches a temperature of 254° (123°C) – check with a sugar thermometer. Remove from the heat and blend in the wheat, stirring with a wooden spatula. Pour the mixture onto a nonstick baking sheet, or one covered with baking parchment. Bake in the oven for 8-10 minutes until lightly browned.

Cut the hot nougatine with a 3-inch (8 cm) cookie cutter. Mold each round of nougatine around the base of a small coffee cup to create a goblet shape. Leave to harden.

Roll out 5 ounces (150 g) shortcrust dough to a thickness of ⅛ inch (3 mm). Store the rest of the dough in the refrigerator to use another time. Butter 4 cake pans 3 inches (8 cm) in diameter and ¾ inch (1.5 cm) deep. Fill them with dough, prick the bases with a fork and bake in the oven for 12 minutes at 425°F (220°C; gas mark 7) until golden. Turn out and leave to cool on a rack.

Prepare the puffed wheat cookies: turn the oven up to 475°F (250°C; gas mark 9).

Mix the wheat and sugar. Melt the butter and stir into the wheat mixture with a wooden spatula. Arrange 4 cookie cutters 3 inches (8 cm) in diameter, to use as templates, on a baking sheet lined with baking parchment. Spoon the cookie mixture into the cutters. Remove the cutters and bake in the oven for 5 minutes until the cookies begin to caramelize, then leave to cool.

Assemble the tartlets. Scrub the lemon and lime under warm running water and dry them. Grate the lemon and lime zest and stir half the grated zest into the marmalade. Fill each pastry case with marmalade with a crisp puffed wheat cookie on top. Place a dab of unsweetened whipped cream in the center of each cookie and arrange the nougatine on top. Decorate with a rosette of whipped cream and the remaining lemon and lime zest. Surround the tartlets with a stream of marmalade juice.

4 SERVINGS

SWEET SHORTCRUST PASTRY
- 1 ½ sticks (140 g) unsalted butter, softened
- 1 generous cup (110 g) confectioners' sugar
- 1 ⅔ cups (250 g) flour
- 1 pinch salt, 1 egg plus 1 egg yolk

GRAPE MARMALADE
- 2 pounds (1 kg) Champagne grapes or 1 pound (500 g) black seedless grapes
- ½ cup (10 cl) red table wine

WHEAT NOUGATINE
- 1 ounce (30 g) glucose, scant ½ cup (90 g) sugar
- ¾ stick (75 g) salted butter
- 4 tablespoons milk
- ½ teaspoon apple pectin (optional)
- 1 cup (90 g) coarsely crushed wheat

CRISP PUFFED WHEAT COOKIES
- 2 ounces (50 g) unsweetened puffed wheat
- ½ cup (100 g) unsalted butter
- ½ cup (100 g) sugar

TO FINISH
- ½ cup (10 cl) whipped cream
- 1 lemon, 1 lime

SPECIAL UTENSILS
- 1 cookie cutter, 3 inches (8 cm) in diameter
- 4 cake pans 3 inches (8 cm) in diameter
- 4 round cookie cutters 3 inches (8 cm) in diameter, to use as templates

Wine suggestion: pink champagne, such as Pommery, Cuvée Louise Pommery.

Mascarpone Ravioli with Spinach, Chanterelles and Parmesan Cheese

BY ALESSANDRO STRATTA

Spread half the ravioli wrappers on the work surface. Cut them into quarters. Place a little mascarpone in the middle of each square.

Whisk the eggs in a cup, adding a little salt. Brush beaten egg around the mascarpone. Cut the remaining ravioli wrappers into quarters and lay one quarter on top of each portion of mascarpone and press firmly around the edges to seal.

Cut the ravioli with a round cookie cutter 1 ¼ inches (3.5 mm) in diameter. Arrange the ravioli on a lightly floured baking sheet and refrigerate.

Clean the chanterelles and wash them quickly. Wash the spinach. Peel and crush the garlic clove.
Heat a little olive oil in a skillet. When the oil is hot, add the chanterelles and sauté over a medium heat until all the liquid has evaporated.

Add the spinach and garlic, and sauté for 3 minutes. Add 1 tablespoon (10 g) butter. Season with salt and pepper and sprinkle with chives. Keep hot.

Bring a large saucepan of water to a boil. Add coarse salt. Place the ravioli in the boiling water and cook for 2 minutes until they float to the surface. Drain and transfer to a saucepan with 2 tablespoons chicken stock and 1 level tablespoon (10 g) butter. Toss the ravioli in stock and butter. Adjust the seasoning.

Arrange a bed of spinach and some of the chanterelles in the center of each plate. Arrange the ravioli on top, with the rest of the chanterelles. Add the Parmesan shavings and drizzle with a little chicken stock. Serve hot, garnished with chervil leaves.

4 SERVINGS

- 1 pack ravioli wrappers
  3 ½ inches (8 cm) square
- 1 cup plus 2 level tablespoons
  mascarpone
- 2 eggs
- Flour
- 4 ½ ounces (120 g) chanterelles
- 4 ounces (100 g) young spinach
- 1 garlic clove
- Olive oil
- 2 level tablespoons (20 g)
  unsalted butter
- 1 teaspoon minced chives
- 4 tablespoons light chicken stock
  (see page 130)
- 2 tablespoons Parmesan shavings
- 2 tablespoons chervil leaves
- Salt, freshly ground pepper
- Coarse salt

SPECIAL UTENSILS

- 1 round cookie cutter,
  1 ¼ inches (3.5 mm)
  in diameter.

*Wine suggestion: a red Burgundy,
such as Clos-de-Vougeot grand
cru, Domaine Bertagna.*

Bresse Chicken Cooked in a Pig's Bladder, with Albufera Sauce and Stewed Vegetables

BY ALAIN DUCASSE

2 SERVINGS

FROM THE MARKET
- **1 Bresse chicken, weighing 3 ½ pounds (1.6 kg)**
- **1 pig's bladder**
- **1 ¼ tablespoons (15 g) foie gras fat**
- **½ tablespoon cognac**
- **1 tablespoon Madeira**
- **1 tablespoon white port**
- **1 generous ounce (30 g) raw white Alba truffle**
- **Fine salt**

Clean the pig's bladder 48 hours in advance. Leave the bladder under running water for 48 hours, or soak it in a bowl of water, changing the water every 2 hours. Rub with fingers from time to time to loosen any impurities.

Prepare the chicken: remove all but one inch of the feet and hold the feet over a flame until the skin turns brown, then remove the brown skin with a knife. Remove the nerves from the legs and trim off the wing tips. Clean the chicken, discard the fat and remove the giblets.

Clean the liver (carefully removing all traces of gall) and the heart. Mince the liver and heart together. Melt 1 teaspoon *foie gras* fat in a skillet, and seal the minced giblets over a high heat. Strain through a sieve to remove excess fat and leave to cool. Season the inside of the chicken with 1 teaspoon (5 g) sea salt. Place the cold giblets inside the chicken, and truss.

Drain the pig's bladder and slip the trussed chicken inside. Add the cognac, Madeira, white port, the rest of the *foie gras* fat and salt. Tie the pig's bladder as closely as possible around the chicken, securing the end with kitchen twine.

Heat 2 quarts (2 l) water in a large stew pot. As soon as the water boils, add the pig's bladder, cover and simmer very gently for 1 hour. After 1 hour, remove from the pot and leave to rest for 20 minutes.

Prepare the Albufera sauce: preheat the oven to 275°F (140°C; gas mark 1). Chop the chicken carcass into large pieces. Place the pieces in a cast iron pot, add the chicken stock, and cook in the oven for 1 ½ hours.

Meanwhile, pour 1 tablespoon white port, 1 tablespoon Madeira and ½ tablespoon cognac into a saucepan. Reduce by three-quarters and reserve. Rub the *foie gras* and butter through a sieve with the aid of a spatula.

After 1 ½ hours, strain the contents of the pot through a chinois (or fine sieve) and reduce the liquid by half over a medium heat to reinforce the flavor. Stir in the reserved spirits, cream and truffle *jus*. Stir in the butter and *foie gras*, whisking with a balloon whisk or spatula. Season with sea salt and freshly ground pepper, and add a few drops of white truffle oil. Stir to obtain a creamy sauce, then strain. Check the seasoning and, if necessary, add a few drops of lemon juice.

Prepare the vegetables: peel the carrots and turnips, removing the tops. Remove the outer stalks of the celery heart, then cut in half, and trim to a length 3 inches (7 cm). Wash all the vegetables.

Cut off the roots and green portion of the leeks. Peel off the outer layer of white portion and wash carefully. Peel the green onions, removing the roots and green tops.

Albufera sauce
- **1 chicken carcass**
- **1 ¼ cups (30 cl) chicken stock**
- **1 tablespoon white port**
- **1 tablespoon Madeira**
- **½ tablespoon cognac**
- **2 tablespoons (30 g) unsalted butter**
- **2 ounces (50 g) cooked duck foie gras (see method)**
- **½ cup (10 cl) light cream**
- **1 tablespoon (2 cl) truffle jus**
- **A few drops truffle oil**
- **Lemon juice**
- **Sea salt**
- **Freshly ground pepper**

Stewed vegetables
- **2 carrots, with tops**
- **2 turnips, with tops**
- **1 celery heart, halved**
- **2 medium leeks**
- **2 whole green onions**
- **1 quart (1 l) chicken stock**
- **½ stick (50 g) unsalted butter**

● Choose the best quality vegetables and a Bresse chicken weighing 3 ½ pounds (1.6 kg).

● Slip the stuffed and seasoned chicken into the pig's bladder.

● Tie the bladder as closely as possible around the chicken with kitchen twine.

● Chop the chicken carcass into pieces and place in a cast iron pot.

● Pour the chicken stock over the pieces of carcass and cook in the oven.

● Reduce the port, Madeira and cognac by three-quarters in a saucepan.

● Using a spatula, rub the duck *foie gras* and butter through a sieve.

● Add the cream, reduced spirits and truffle *jus* to the reduced stock.

Cook the vegetables: bring the chicken stock to a boil in a saucepan. Add the carrots and leeks. Cover and cook for 10 minutes. Then add the turnips, celery and green onions. Remove the vegetables from the stock with a slotted spoon as soon as they are cooked, checking them with the point of a knife.

Reduce the stock over a high heat until a little under a cup (20 cl) remains. Whisk 4 tablespoons butter into the stock, a small piece at a time. Reheat the vegetables in the thickened stock, gently shaking the saucepan so that the vegetables are coated in stock.

While the stock is reducing, bring a saucepan of water to a boil, add the chicken and reheat in simmering water for 15 minutes.

● Whisk with a balloon whisk.

● Stir the butter and *foie gras* into the sauce, using the balloon whisk.

● Stir, strain and, if necessary, add a little lemon juice. Season.

● Remove all but 1 ¼ inches (3 cm) of the carrot tops. Scrape the carrots with a paring knife.

Drain the pig's bladder, remove the twine, cut the bladder open and remove the chicken. Untie the chicken and cut into four pieces. Remove the skin and wings: only the breast is used for this dish.

Place the chicken breasts on a rack over a roasting pan and coat them generously with Albufera sauce. The surplus sauce will run into the pan.

Arrange 1 carrot, 1 turnip, half a celery heart, 1 leek and 1 green onion on each plate. On top, place a chicken breast coated with sauce and grate white truffle over the sauce. Serve the rest of the sauce separately.

Wine suggestion: a white wine from the Rhône Valley, such as Châteauneuf-du-Pape, Domaine le Pegeau, 1990.

● Prepare the leeks: cut off the roots and remove the first layer.

● Add the carrots and leeks to the boiling chicken stock.

● Place the chicken breasts on a grid over a roasting pan and coat them with Albufera sauce.

● Arrange a chicken breast on each plate. Grate white truffle over each portion just before serving.

66 *TARTUFI* ARE ROUNDED AND IRREGULARLY SHAPED. THE SKIN IS SMOOTH, THE COLOR OF OLD IVORY, CHANGING FROM PALE BEIGE WHEN FIRST PICKED AND YELLOWING WITH AGE. THE FLESH IS PINKISH BEIGE WITH PALER, ALMOST WHITE VEINS, AND GIVES OFF A UNIQUE FRAGRANCE. 99

CONTENTS

● Alain Ducasse ●
Bresse Chicken Cooked in a Pig's Bladder, with Albufera Sauce and Stewed Vegetables

Tartufi di Alba are such a powerful seasoning that they can only be used with the simplest products with the "purest" flavors: hence the idea of chicken poached in a pig's bladder and stewed vegetables. At the same time, truffles need fat to fix their fragrance, which is why they are accompanied here by Albufera sauce (whose name derives from a classic chicken garnish based on *foie gras* and truffles) which helps to create harmony between the different ingredients.

● Franck Cerutti ●
Mona Lisa Potato Gnocchi
with Alba Truffles

Tartufi di Alba are very much at home with starchy ingredients – in Italy they are traditionally served with pasta, risotto and gnocchi – but they also need fat to fix and develop their unique flavor. In this recipe, the fat is derived from three different sources: butter with sage and Parmesan cheese to coat the gnocchi, the bed of veal *jus* blended with whipped cream, and plain veal *jus* to enhance the taste. The garnish of fine *tartufi* shavings gives off maximum fragrance.

• Jean-Louis Nomicos •
Caramelized Spit-roasted Winter Vegetables, Arugula and Grated White Truffle

The lightly acidulated chicken stock and the olive oil dressing on the arugula provide the necessary fat to enable the *tartufi di Alba* to develop their flavor to the full. The arugula offers a piquant counterpoint to the powerful fragrance of the white truffle. The twice-cooked vegetables have a crunchy but, at the same time, melting consistency to contrast with the crisp arugula.

• Sylvain Portay •
Poached Egg topped with Grated White Truffle, with Ragout of Calf's Foot and Veal Sweetbreads, Baby Onions and Horns of Plenty

Here, the *tartufi di Alba* are treated in the French style and used like black truffles. The egg yolk provides the element of fat needed to highlight the truffle flavor (reinforced by the addition of the truffle parings to the ragout of sweetbreads, calf's foot and mushroom). There is a pleasing contrast between the firm textures of the sweetbreads, horns of plenty and onions, and the crunchiness of the fried brioche all bound with the fragrant egg yolk.

• Jean-François Piège •
Veal Sweetbreads, Swiss Chard au gratin and Grated *Tuber magnatum pico*

Tartufi di Alba were made to be a luxurious condiment. They are virtually "uncookable" and so very Italian, and difficult to adapt to traditional French cuisine. Even so, their flavor is incomparable and irreplaceable. This dish was inspired by the Piedmontese custom of combining the *tuber magnatum pico* with a few drops of hazelnut butter which in turn reflects the taste of gently fried sweetbreads.

• Alessandro Stratta •
Scallops with Celery Root and White Truffles

The marriage between *tartufi di Alba* and celery root has become something of a classic, as has the combination of truffles and scallops whose sweet, almost sugary flavor blends so well with strong-tasting vegetables and seasonings. The liquid of the vegetable ragout, prepared like a risotto, and the oil used to dress the celery root salad provide the fat needed to highlight the subtle taste of truffles. The texture of the celery root, meanwhile, presents a contrast to the soft, delicate scallop meat.

Mona Lisa Potato Gnocchi with Alba Truffles

BY FRANCK CERUTTI

Prepare the gnocchi, using, if possible, potatoes grown in the mountains: wash the potatoes and place them in a saucepan of cold water. Season with coarse salt. Bring to a boil, then cover and cook for 25 minutes. When the potatoes are cooked, peel them and pass them through a sieve or potato ricer onto a marble chopping board. Sprinkle with ½ cup (80 g) flour.

Break the egg into a cup, beat with a fork then add to the potatoes with a pinch of sea salt and a little freshly grated nutmeg. Blend thoroughly, gradually adding about ⅛ cup (20 g) flour to obtain a ball of smooth dough.

Shape the dough into long sausages about ¾ inch (1.5 cm) in diameter and cut into 1-inch (2-cm) pieces. Roll each piece into a ball between the palms of the hands, then press with the back of a fork to produce a grooved effect.

Bring a wide saucepan of water to a boil and add salt. Turn the heat down and place the gnocchi in the boiling water. Remove them from the water with a slotted spoon as soon as they float to the surface and plunge immediately into a bowl of iced water.

Drain the gnocchi in a colander and dry them on a cloth. Coat them with a little oil to prevent them sticking together and place them in a bowl. Gnocchi can be prepared in advance.

Finish the dish: whip the cream until it peaks and doubles in volume.
Scrub the truffle under cold, running water.

Bring a saucepan of water to a boil and add salt. Plunge the gnocchi in the boiling water to reheat them. Pour ½ cup (10 cl) chicken stock into a 10-inch (25 cm) skillet. Add the sage and butter and bring to a boil. Drain the gnocchi and tip them into the skillet and roll them in the sauce. Sprinkle with Parmesan, turning the skillet round and round in a clockwise direction so that the gnocchi are well coated.

Heat the veal *jus*, and divide into two portions. Add 3 tablespoons whipped cream to one portion and pour onto hot plates. Arrange the gnocchi on top and surround them with a few drops of the remaining veal *jus*. At the table, grate generously with white truffle shavings, using a Japanese mandolin.

4 SERVINGS

- 1 generous pound (500 g) yellow-fleshed Mona Lisa potatoes
- 1 white truffle, weighing 2 ounces (50 g)
- ⅔ cup (100 g) flour
- 1 new-laid egg
- Nutmeg
- Oil
- ½ cup (10 cl) light cream
- ½ cup (10 cl) light chicken stock (see page 130)
- 4 sage leaves
- ½ stick unsalted butter
- ¾ cup (80 g) grated Parmesan cheese
- ¼ cup (5 cl) veal jus (see page 130); rabbit jus may be used instead
- Coarse salt
- Fine salt

SPECIAL UTENSILS
- 1 Japanese mandolin

Wine suggestion: a white Italian wine from Piedmont, such as Barolo or Barbaresco, A. Gaja.

Caramelized Spit-roasted Winter Vegetables, Arugula and Grated White Truffle

BY JEAN-LOUIS NOMICOS

Cut the pumpkin into 1 ½ inch (4-cm) rounds, ¾ inch (1.5 cm) thick. Arrange the pumpkin rounds on a plate, drizzle with olive oil, sprinkle with salt, pepper and crushed garlic and add a small piece of bacon rind. Cover with aluminum foil and bake in the oven at its very lowest setting for1 ½ hours. The pumpkin should remain slightly crisp.

Prepare the vegetable stock: peel the onion and carrot. Bring the chicken stock to a boil. Add the onion, carrot, *bouquet garni* and peppercorns. Cook for 20 minutes.

Remove the rind and cartilage from the bacon. Place the bacon in a saucepan of cold water, bring to a boil and simmer for 10 minutes. Drain the bacon and rinse under cold running water. Add it to the vegetable stock and simmer gently while preparing the rest of the vegetables.

Peel the artichoke stalks. Trim off the points of the leaves and remove the lower leaves with a small, sharp knife. Remove the choke with a teaspoon.

Cut the celery root into isosceles triangles ¾ inch (1.5 cm) thick, measuring 2 inches (5 cm) either side and 1 ¼ inches (3 cm) along the base.

Peel the beets. Cut into cylinders 1 inch (2.5 cm) in diameter and 1 ½ inches (4 cm) long. Peel the scallions. Wash and scrub the potatoes, removing any blemishes. Trim off the arugula stalks and wash and dry the leaves.

Place the potatoes in the stock, and cook for 15 minutes. Cook the celery root, scallions and then the artichokes for about 10 minutes each. The vegetables should not be completely cooked, as they will also be spit-roasted. Check them with the point of a knife and place on a bed of ice as they are removed from the saucepan.

Cut the bacon into pieces ¾ inch (1.5 cm) thick and 2 ¼ inches (6 cm) long. Loosely thread the bacon and all the vegetables, including the beets and pumpkin onto skewers. Brush lightly with chicken *jus*. Place the skewers on a baking sheet under the grill, 6-8 inches (15-20 cm) from the heat source. Brown and caramelize for about 15 minutes, basting frequently with chicken *jus* and turning several times.

Arrange the vegetables attractively on the plates, seasoning the chicken *jus* lightly with lemon juice. Dress the arugula with olive oil and arrange it on top of the vegetables. Add shavings of white truffle, preferably using a truffle mandolin, at the very last minute.

4 SERVINGS

- 1 ½ ounces (40 g) white truffle
- ¼ pumpkin
- Olive oil
- 1 garlic clove
- 4 small purple Provençal
  artichokes
- 1 celery root
- 2 cooked beets
- 4 scallions
- 4 Ratte or other yellow-fleshed
  waxy potatoes
- 2 ounces (50 g) wild arugula
- ½ cup (10 cl) chicken jus
  (adapted from the recipe for veal
  jus, page 130)
- 1 lemon
- Salt, freshly ground pepper

VEGETABLE STOCK

- 1 white onion
- 1 carrot
- 2 quarts (2 l) chicken stock
- 1 bouquet garni
- 10 black peppercorns
- 14 ounces (400 g) bacon,
  in one piece

SPECIAL UTENSILS

- 4 metal skewers
- 1 truffle mandolin

*Wine suggestion: a white wine
from the Rhône Valley, such as
Châteauneuf-du-Pape, Vieilles
Vignes, Château de Beaucastel,
1996.*

Veal Sweetbreads, Swiss Chard au gratin and Grated *Tuber magnatum pico*

BY JEAN-FRANÇOIS PIÈGE

Prepare the garnish: separate the ribs and leaves of the Swiss chard. Remove the strings from the ribs, neatly trim the ends and edges and place in cold water with a few drops of lemon juice.

Soften the bone marrow in a skillet with a little olive oil. Drain the chard ribs. Toss them in the fat and cook gently for a few minutes without allowing them to take color. Bring the chicken stock to a boil and add just enough to cover the ribs. Dice the butter and add to the skillet. Cover and simmer gently for 15 minutes. The ribs should be soft and coated in their natural juices. Transfer to a dish and leave to cool.

Remove the tough veins from the chard leaves. Bring a large saucepan of salted water to a boil and cook the leaves for 5-8 minutes. Drain, refresh in iced water, then drain on a cloth.

Cut the ribs and leaves into rectangles of equal size. Arrange the ribs and leaves in an alternating pattern on a baking sheet lined with baking parchment. Cut out two half-moon shapes using a round 5-inch (12-cm) cookie cutter.

Remove the stalks from the horns of plenty, wash in plenty of water and drain. Sauté in a skillet over a high heat with a little *foie gras* fat. Add seasoning.

Prepare the veal sweetbreads: remove the membrane, using a knife with a flexible blade. Cut the sweetbreads into a neat oval shape. Season with fine salt. Heat the butter in a skillet. When it froths, add the sweetbreads and cook over a medium heat for about 15 minutes, until golden.

Squeeze the lemon. Remove the sweetbreads from the skillet with a slotted spoon. Skim off some of the fat and deglaze the skillet with the lemon juice. Return the sweetbreads to the skillet and turn them in the pan juices. Leave to rest for 5 minutes.

Preheat the oven to 300°F (150°C; gas mark 2). Heat the half-moons of Swiss chard on their baking sheet for 3 minutes. Spoon their juices over them to give a glazed finish. Reheat the sweetbreads for 3 minutes. Reheat the veal *jus* over a low heat.

Using a wide spatula, transfer a half moon of chard to each plate. Place the horns of plenty and sweetbreads on top. Cover with veal *jus* and garnish with grated truffle. Serve immediately.

2 SERVINGS

- 2 veal sweetbreads, each weighing 8 ounces (220 g), blanched
- 1 ½ ounces (40 g) tuber magnatum pico white truffles
- 1 stick (100 g) clarified unsalted butter (see page 171)
- 1 Menton lemon
- ½ cup (10 cl) veal jus (see page 130)
- Fine salt
- Freshly ground pepper

GARNISH
- 1 bunch Swiss chard
- Lemon juice
- 2 ounces (50 g) bone marrow
- ½ cup (10 cl) olive oil
- 2 cups (50 cl) light chicken stock (see page 130)
- 1 stick (100 g) unsalted butter
- 7 ounces (200 g) horn of plenty mushrooms
- Foie gras fat

SPECIAL UTENSILS
- 1 cookie cutter, 5 inches (12 cm) in diameter

Wine suggestion: a white wine from the Rhône Valley, such as Châteauneuf-du-Pape, Clos des Pontifes, J. Marchand, 1995.

Poached Egg topped with Grated White Truffle, with Ragout of Calf's Foot and Veal Sweetbreads, Baby Onions and Horns of Plenty

BY SYLVAIN PORTAY

Carefully clean the truffle with a soft brush under running water to remove every trace of grit. Dry the truffle and wrap it in absorbent paper to keep it dry.

Peel the baby onions. Heat ½ tablespoon olive oil in a skillet. Fry the onions briefly in the hot oil, season and add 5 tablespoons chicken stock, scraping the base of the pan with a spatula. Turn the heat down low, then cover and simmer for 15 minutes, until tender. If necessary, add a little more stock from time to time. Remove the onions and rinse the skillet.

Carefully wash the mushrooms and dry them thoroughly. Peel and crush the garlic cloves. Heat ½ tablespoon oil in the skillet. Add half the garlic and all the mushrooms. Season with salt and pepper. When all the mushroom liquid has evaporated, add 1 tablespoon (10 g) butter, stir and remove from the heat.

Preheat the oven to 350°F (180°C; gas mark 4). Season the sweetbreads. Heat a little olive oil and 1 tablespoon (10 g) butter in an ovenproof pan and gently fry the sweetbreads for a few minutes. Add the carrot, celery, scallion and the rest of the garlic. Moisten with the white wine and cook until all the wine has evaporated. Add enough veal *jus* to half cover the sweetbreads. Cover with baking parchment and cook in the oven for 20 minutes. Leave to cool.

Cut the truffle into a regular rounded shape with a small knife. Mash the parings with a fork.

Bring a large saucepan of water to a boil. Add the vinegar. Reduce the heat and poach the eggs for 2 minutes in the simmering water. Transfer the eggs from the saucepan to a plate with a slotted spoon.

Cut the brioche slices with a 1 ½-inch (4-cm) cookie cutter. Spread with butter and toast quickly on both sides under the grill.

Dice the calf's foot. Cut the sweetbreads into ½-inch (1 cm) dice. In a skillet, mix the calf's foot, sweetbreads, sweetbread juices, mushrooms and baby onions. Cook over a low heat for 1-2 minutes, binding with 2 tablespoons (20 g) butter and a little olive oil. Adjust the seasoning and add the mashed truffle parings.

Carefully return the poached eggs to the simmering water and cook for 1 minute more. Remove from the water with a slotted spoon and drain on a cloth.

Place the toasted brioche in the center of each heated plate, with a poached egg on top. Surround with the ragout and sauce. Sprinkle with very fine slivers of truffle, cut on a Japanese mandolin. Drizzle the truffles with olive oil, a little fine salt and freshly ground pepper. Serve immediately.

4 SERVINGS

- 2 ounces (50 g) white Alba truffles
- 5 ounces (150 g) veal sweetbreads, blanched
- 8 baby onions
- 4 tablespoons (5 cl) olive oil
- ½ cup (12 cl) light chicken stock (see page 130)
- 4 ounces (100 g) horn of plenty mushrooms or chanterelles
- 4 garlic cloves
- 4 level tablespoons (50 g) butter
- ⅓ cup (50 g) carrot, finely diced
- ½ stick celery, finely diced
- 1 scallion, minced
- ½ cup (12 cl) white wine
- 6 tablespoons (10 cl) veal jus (see page 130)
- 2 tablespoons vinegar
- 4 new-laid eggs
- 4 slices stale brioche, ¾ inch (2 cm) thick
- 1 calf's foot, cooked
- Fine salt
- Freshly ground pepper
- Fine salt

SPECIAL UTENSILS

- 1 cookie cutter, 1 ½ inches (4 cm) in diameter
- 1 Japanese mandolin

Wine suggestion: a white Burgundy, such as Mâcon-Clessé, Domaine de la Bongran, Jean Thévenet, 1990.

Scallops with Celery Root and White Truffles

BY ALESSANDRO STRATTA

Prepare the celery root ragout: peel the celery root and cut into ⅛ inch (3 mm) dice. Peel, degerm and mince the garlic. Clean and finely dice the leek. Peel and wash the potatoes and cut them into ⅛ inch (3 cm dice).

Melt 1 ½ tablespoons (20 g) butter in a skillet, then add the garlic and leek. Soften over a low heat for 5 minutes. Season with salt and pepper. Add the diced celery root and stir for a further 2-3 minutes.

Add the potatoes and stir so that they are well coated with butter. Cook for 3 minutes. Add the wine, scraping the base of the pan with a spatula. Allow the wine to evaporate, taking care that the vegetables do not stick to the pan.

Bring the chicken stock to a boil. Add just enough stock to the skillet to cover the vegetables. Simmer over a low heat. When all the liquid has evaporated, add more stock and evaporate over a low heat, then add the remaining stock. When all this has evaporated, the potatoes should be almost cooked. Add the crème fraîche and the rest of the butter. Simmer over a low heat, like a risotto, until the vegetables are *al dente*. Check the seasoning.

Prepare the garnish: cut a firm, white celery heart in half lengthwise and cut into fine julienne on a mandolin. Whisk the lemon juice and olive oil together and pour the mixture over the celery. Season with salt and pepper, then stir in the minced chives.

Heat the oil to a temperature of 350°F (180°C). Peel the piece of celery root and cut into 4 thin slices to make chips. Fry for a few seconds in hot fat then drain.

Cook the scallops. Remove the beard and the small white muscle. Rinse the scallops and wipe dry with absorbent paper. Season.

Pour the oil into a skillet. When the oil is hot, brown the scallops for 30 seconds, then add the butter. Turn the scallops in butter, cooking them for 2 minutes in all, until they are opaque in the middle. Remove from the heat and leave to rest for 1 minute.

Spoon 2 tablespoons celery root ragout onto each plate and arrange 3 scallops on top. Arrange a little celery salad on the scallops. Surround with hot chicken *jus* and finish with a celery root chip. Season with fine salt. Grate the white truffle over the finished dish and serve hot.

4 SERVINGS

- 12 scallops, shelled
- 4 ounces (100 g) white truffles
- 1 teaspoon olive oil
- 1 ½ tablespoons (20 g) unsalted butter
- 2 tablespoons chicken jus (adapted from recipe for veal jus, page 130)
- Fine salt
- Salt, freshly ground white pepper

CELERY ROOT RAGOUT

- 7 ounces (200 g) celery root
- 4 garlic cloves
- 1 leek, white portion only
- 2 starchy potatoes
- 4 tablespoons (60 g) unsalted butter
- ½ cup (12 cl) dry white wine
- 3 cups (75 cl) light chicken stock (see page 130)
- 4 tablespoons crème fraîche

GARNISH

- 1 large or 2 small celery hearts
- 1 teaspoon lemon juice
- 2 teaspoons virgin olive oil
- 1 tablespoon minced chives
- 1 piece celery root
- Oil for deep frying

Wine suggestion: a white wine from the Loire Valley, such as Savannières "Roche aux moines", Château de Chamboureau.

Sea Bass Steaks with Leeks, Potatoes and Truffles

BY ALAIN DUCASSE

4 SERVINGS

FROM THE MARKET
- **1 sea bass, weighing 6 ½ pounds (3 kg)**
- **1 potato**
- **1 leek**
- **½ stick butter**
- **Olive oil**
- **Sea salt**

Fish sauce
- **2 scallions**
- **2 garlic cloves**
- **1 fennel bulb**
- **1 tablespoon olive oil**
- **6 tablespoons (70 g) butter**
- **½ cup (10 cl) white wine**
- **2 sprigs dried fennel**
- **10 coriander seeds**
- **10 black pepper corns**
- **Pinch piment d'Espelette (hot pepper from the Basque region) or cayenne pepper**
- **2 tablespoons crème fraîche, well chilled**

Prepare the savory beef stock: place the beef chunks in a stew pot with enough water to cover, season with salt and bring to a boil. Skim off the fat and scum. Add all the vegetables and spices. Simmer, uncovered, over a low heat for 3 ½ hours. Skim from time to time, removing all the fat. When cooked, strain the stock and refrigerate.

Prepare the bass: scale and clean the fish and rinse under cold running water. To fillet the fish, place it flat on the work surface and cut the skin along the backbone from head to tail. Cut through the backbone just below the head. Cut into the flesh along the backbone, keeping the knife flat against the bone to detach the fillet completely, lifting the flesh. Remove the first fillet and repeat the same process on the other side.

To skin the fillets, lay the fillet flat, skin side down, on the work surface. Pull away ½-¾ inch (1-2 cm) of skin from the tail end, grasp firmly in the left hand, insert the cutting edge of the knife between skin and flesh at a slight angle to the skin, moving towards the head, sliding the knife gently back and forth. For this process, use a filleting knife with a long, thin, flexible blade.

Check that no bones remain by passing the hand over the flesh, removing any remaining bones with tweezers. Remove the blood clots and fat. Reserve the head to use in the sauce. Divide the fish into 4 steaks, each weighing about 5 ½ ounces (160 g).

Prepare the fish sauce: to clean the fish head, leave it under running water for several minutes. Cut in half. Peel and slice the scallions. Peel, halve, degerm and crush the garlic cloves. Cut off the hard base of the fennel bulb and discard any tough stalks. Cut the fennel into thin slices.

Heat 1 tablespoon olive oil in a cast iron pot. Add ¼ stick (20 g) butter. Place the fish head in the hot fat and fry for a few minutes until brown all over, turning frequently. Add the minced scallions, crushed garlic and fresh fennel. Cover and simmer over a low heat for 5 minutes to soften the vegetables. Deglaze the pot with white wine, scraping the base of the pan with a spatula, and reduce by half over a medium heat. Pour 2 cups (50 cl) beef stock into the pot. Add the dried fennel, coriander, peppercorns and *piment d'Espelette* (hot pepper from the Basque region), or cayenne pepper. Simmer, uncovered, for 45 minutes over a low heat. When ready, strain through a chinois (or fine sieve). Reserve the liquid and discard the solid ingredients.

Clarify the butter: gently melt the butter in a saucepan, leave to rest, then skim. Pour the butter into a bowl leaving the whey in the pan. Because it keeps very well in the refrigerator, it is worth preparing 1 cup (200 g) of clarified butter at a time. Clarified butter has the special virtue of tolerating quite high temperatures without turning black.

Prepare the garnish: peel and wash the two waxy potatoes, cut into 36 triangles (9 per serving), ⅛ inch (3 mm) thick, and ¾ inch (2 cm) along each side. Heat ½ cup (100 g) clarified butter in a skillet to a temperature of about 175° F (80°C), which is just under boiling point for butter. Check visually or with a kitchen thermometer. Place the potato triangles in the hot butter and cook for 45 minutes, stirring frequently. Make sure that the butter temperature never exceeds 185°F (85°C). Season with sea salt.

Garnish
- **2 large waxy potatoes**
- **8 medium leeks**
- **7 ounces (200 g) truffles**
- **½ cup (100 g) clarified unsalted butter (see method)**
- **Sea salt**

Savory beef stock
- **6 ½ pounds (3 kg) stewing beef (such as chuck, short plate, rib or brisket), cut into chunks**
- **1 bouquet garni**
- **3 carrots, peeled**
- **2 onions, peeled and studded with 3 or 4 cloves**
- **2 onions, halved and dry-fried to a golden color**
- **5 garlic cloves, unpeeled**
- **4 sticks celery**
- **7 ounces (200 g) leeks, green portions only**
- **Sea salt**

Special utensils
- **Kitchen thermometer**

● Take a 6 ½-pound (3-kg) sea bass, waxy potatoes and 7 ounces (200 g) truffles.

● Scale, clean and fillet the fish. Discard fat and blood clots.

● Soften the fish head in a cast iron pot with the scallions, fennel and crushed garlic cloves.

● Pour the savory beef stock into the pot. Add the seasonings and piment d'Espelette.

● Cut the potatoes into 36 triangles ⅛ inch (3 mm) thick, and ¾ inch (2 cm) along each side.

● Heat the clarified butter to 175°F (80°C), which is just below boiling point for butter. Make sure it does not boil.

● Add the potato triangles to the hot butter and cook for 45 minutes.

● Cut the white part of the leek into thick diagonal pieces.

Remove the roots, the first layer and the green part of the leeks. Wash and cut into 36 chunks (9 per serving), sliced at an angle. Bring a saucepan of water to a boil, add salt, then add the leeks and cook for 20 minutes. Drain, refresh under cold running water, and reserve.

Cut the truffles into triangles the same size as the potatoes. Chop the parings with a knife.

Cook the sea bass steaks: preheat the oven to 350°F (180°C; gas mark 4). Peel and wash the potato. Clean and carefully wash the leek and cut into chunks.

Brush the steaks with olive oil. Season with sea salt. Heat an ovenproof skillet, add the fish steaks and brown over a medium heat for 2 minutes each side. Add the sliced potato, ½ stick (50 g) butter and ½ cup (10 cl) beef stock. Place the skillet in the oven and cook the fish for 8 minutes, basting frequently with the pan juices in order to glaze the steaks.

● Cook the leeks in boiling salted water for 20 minutes.

● Cut the truffles into triangles ⅛ inch (3 mm) thick, and ¾ (2 cm) along each side.

● Brush each sea bass steak with olive oil. Add seasoning.

● Cook the fish with butter, rich beef stock, potato and leek.

Heat the fish sauce and reduce to a creamy consistency. Whip the crème fraîche. Stir 4 tablespoons (50 g) butter into the sauce, and finally add the whipped crème fraîche and truffles, but do not stir.

If necessary, reheat the vegetables over a low heat.

Arrange the sliced leeks in a circle on the plates, with potato and truffle triangles in between. Cover with fish sauce. Place one sea bass steak in the center of each plate. Serve the rest of the sauce separately.

Wine suggestion: a white wine from the Touraine, such as a Vouvray sec, Domaine de la Fontainerie, C. Dhoye-Deruet, 1996.

● Baste regularly with the pan juices to coat the fish.

● Reduce the fish sauce to a creamy consistency.

● Add the whipped crème fraîche and the truffle parings but do not stir.

● Arrange the potato and truffle triangles on top of each other. Place the sea bass in the center of the plate.

" THE SEA BASS LIKES WELL-OXYGENATED WATER. IT SWIMS CLOSE TO THE COAST WHERE BREAKERS AND ROLLERS STIR UP THE SEA. A VORACIOUS PREDATOR, IT FEEDS ON SMALL FISH, CRABS AND SQUID. "

CONTENTS

● Alain Ducasse ●
Sea Bass Steaks with Leeks, Potatoes and Truffles

To bring out the best in this most noble of fish, Alain Ducasse chooses a fairly large sea bass. He uses only the white flesh of the fillets in order to keep the flavor as pure as possible and combines it with a truffle-based garnish to provide classic flavor combinations: leek and potato, potato and truffle, leeks and truffle. This is an enriched version of potage *parmentier*, made with beef stock seasoned with *piment d'Espelette* (or cayenne pepper) to enhance the taste of the fish.

● Franck Cerutti ●
Fried Mediterranean Bass,
Prickly Artichokes and Anchovy Toast

This dish sets out to achieve a "wilder" flavor, with the fish only fried on the skin side to capture the tastes of the sea. The melt-in-the-mouth texture of the fish contrasts with the slight crunchiness of the cooked artichokes and the definite bite of the raw ones, harmonized to perfection by the velouté sauce (the pith of the spiny artichoke stalks is very sweet and aromatic). The ingredients of freshly-cooked anchovy toast – capers, anchovies and olives – add some much stronger flavors.

• Jean-Louis Nomicos •
Sea Bass Steaks, Shrimps and
Ratte Potatoes with Caviar

Noble fish served with shrimp sauce and a shrimp garnish is one of the classics of *grande cuisine*. Here the recipe is brought right up to date with an added touch of originality – potatoes dressed with caviar. The shrimps provide the perfect transition between the dramatically contrasting firmness of the sea bass flesh and the Ratte potatoes and the iodized saltiness of the caviar, which serves to highlight the flavor of the fish.

• Sylvain Portay •
Sea Bass and Bacon Tournedos Meunière,
with Green Lentils and Crispy Bacon Garnish

The originality of this dish lies in salting the fish before serving it in the most classic way possible: with lentils garnished in equally classic fashion with carrots, baby onions and parsley. The salting process makes the already firm fish even firmer and denser, providing an interesting contrast with the grainy texture of the lentils. The bacon, presented in two different ways, one to exploit its smoky flavor, the other to add crispness.

• Jean-François Piège •
Sea Bass with Spider Crab
Jus and Seafood Garnish

So noble and elegant is sea bass that only a purely seafood sauce can set it off to its best advantage. The fish is cooked as gently as possible to retain its whiteness. Spider crab, too, has a very delicate flavor, with a subtle tang of iodine, and a soft and smooth texture. The shellfish contribute stronger notes of iodine, as well as saltiness and firm texture. The romaine lettuce lends crispness and the lemon quarters a touch of acidity.

• Alessandro Stratta •
Sea Bass with Mediterranean
Vegetable Salsa and Bouillabaisse Sauce

The Mediterranean vegetable salsa, typical of the Nice region, with its richly varied textures – the smoothness of zucchini and eggplant, the crunch of the pine nuts, the firmness of the capers and softness of the raisins with their tang of vinegar, is the perfect complement to the fish. The fillets are fried only on the skin side so retaining a strong taste of the sea and a firmness and density that contrasts with the different consistencies of the other ingredients. The whole dish is given a distinctively Mediterranean feel by the saffron-flavored bouillabaisse sauce.

Fried Mediterranean Bass, Prickly Artichokes and Anchovy Toast

BY FRANCK CERUTTI

Fillet and skin the fish. Cut the fillets into 4 steaks each weighing about 5 ½ ounces (160 g). Take a generous ounce (30 g) of flesh from the underside of the fish for use in the anchovy rolls and reserve the head for the sauce.

Prepare the sauce: chop the chicken leg into 4 pieces with a cleaver. Dice the bacon. Peel and slice the scallions. Lightly brown the chicken and bacon in a skillet with a little olive oil and 1 ½ tablespoons (20 g) butter. Add the scallions and the unpeeled garlic clove. Soften over a low heat for 5 minutes. Add the fish head and brown gently for 5 minutes. Add enough chicken stock to cover, with the two sorts of pepper. Simmer for 50 minutes, skimming from time to time, then strain.

Remove the artichoke stalks, and peel and slice them. Sauté in 1 tablespoon oil, add enough chicken stock to cover, then cook, covered, until tender, stirring from time to time. If no spiny artichokes (from Italy or southern France) are available, use 4 purple artichoke hearts.

Detach the artichoke hearts and remove the chokes. Cut the hearts into quarters and place them in a bowl of water with lemon juice.

Prepare the anchovy toast: peel and mince the scallion, and fry gently in a little olive oil, until tender. Chop the *gamberoni* (or langoustines), anchovies, the reserved sea bass flesh and capers. Mix with the olive paste and scallion.

Cut the *ficelle* into 4 equal pieces. Toast the bread, then place it in the oven on its lowest setting. The toast should be very dry. Pile anchovy paste onto each piece to create a dome shape.

Cook the fish: rub *a plancha* (metal hotplate placed directly over the gas) or a large skillet with oil-soaked absorbent paper. To avoid burning the fish, heat *the plancha* or skillet – which should be very hot – very slowly over a low heat.
Brush the sea bass steaks with oil and season with salt. Cook very gently for about 15 minutes and only remove them from the heat just before serving.

Meanwhile, dry the artichoke hearts and sauté 6 of them in a little oil for 8-10 minutes. Thinly slice the 4 remaining raw artichokes, and season with olive oil, lemon juice and coarsely chopped parsley.

Heat a skillet and seal the anchovy toast, paste side downwards. Bring the strained sauce base to a boil. Stir in the puréed artichoke stalks. Remove from the heat and add 2 ¾ tablespoons (30 g) butter, a little olive oil and a squeeze of lemon juice. Check the seasoning and stir thoroughly.

Arrange the raw artichoke slices on each plate, place the sea bass steaks on top and surround with the cooked artichokes and velouté sauce. Place a piece of anchovy toast on the side of the plates. Serve piping hot.

4 SERVINGS

- 1 sea bass weighing 6 ½ pounds (3 kg)
- 10 prickly artichokes, with stalks
- Olive oil, lemon juice
- 2 cups (50 cl) light chicken stock (see page 130)
- Coarsely chopped parsley
- Fine salt
- Freshly ground pepper

SAUCE

- 1 chicken leg
- 2 ounces (50 g) streaky bacon or pancetta
- 3 scallions, 1 garlic clove
- ½ stick (50 g) unsalted butter
- 10 black Sarawak (Malaysian) peppercorns
- 6 long Indonesian (Balinese, Jaborandi or Bengal) peppercorns, lemon juice

ANCHOVY CROÛTONS

- 1 scallion
- 4 gamberoni (or langoustines), shelled
- 6 anchovy fillets, preserved in oil
- 1 teaspoon capers
- 1 teaspoon olive paste
- 1 ficelle (French bread stick)

Wine suggestion: a white wine from Provence, such as AOC Palette, Château Simone, René Rougier.

Sea Bass Steaks, Shrimps and Ratte Potatoes with Caviar

BY JEAN-LOUIS NOMICOS

Shell the shrimps and reserve the heads. Reserve 20 whole shrimps for the garnish.

Peel and wash the mushrooms. Cut the white parts of the caps into very small dice. Peel and finely mince the onion. Soften 1 tablespoon of the minced onion in 2 tablespoons (30 g) butter for a few minutes. Add the diced mushrooms, cover and simmer over a low heat until the mushrooms sweat. Remove from the heat.

Coarsely chop the shrimps and add them to the mushrooms with the chopped parsley. Season with salt and pepper.

Gently heat the shrimp heads with 2 tablespoons (30 g) butter for 5 minutes. Add the chicken stock and ¾ cup (20 cl) light cream. Add a sprig of parsley and the trimmings from 2 mushrooms. Increase the heat and cook for 10 minutes. Discard the parsley sprig. Blend in a food processor then pass through a chinois (or fine sieve). The sauce should be an attractive pink color.

Wash the potatoes, place them in a saucepan of cold water and cook for 25 minutes. When the potatoes are cooked, drain them and cut a "lid" a quarter of the way down each potato.

Remove the pulp with a teaspoon. Mash with a fork and blend in ½ stick (50 g) butter, the heavy cream and 1 tablespoon chopped chives. Fill the potatoes with the seasoned pulp and keep hot.

Preheat the oven to 350°F (180°C; gas mark 4). Spread the flesh side of the sea bass steaks with the mushroom and shrimp mixture. Season with salt and pepper.

Grease an ovenproof dish with 1 ½ tablespoons (20 g) butter and arrange the steaks on the dish. Cover and bake in the oven for 12-15 minutes. Drain the steaks and leave them to rest on a rack for 3-4 minutes.

To finish the sauce, add a squeeze of lemon juice and a knob of butter. Stir and gently reheat the sauce, without allowing it to boil.

Melt the slightly salted butter in a small skillet, then quickly sauté the reserved whole shrimps.

Top each potato with a portion of caviar. Arrange the potatoes and sea bass steaks on the plates, surrounded by the sauce. Garnish with sautéed shrimps.

4 SERVINGS

- 4 sea bass steaks, each weighing 5 ounces (150 g) cut from a 9-pound (4-kg) fish, skinned
- 12 ounces (350 g) shrimps (unshelled)
- 1 ounce (24 g) Sevruga caviar
- 4 ounces (100 g) large cultivated mushrooms
- 1 white onion
- 1 ½ sticks (150 g) unsalted butter
- 1 tablespoon coarsely chopped flat-leaf parsley, plus 1 parsley sprig
- ½ cup (10 cl) light chicken stock (see page 130)
- 1 scant cup (20 cl) light cream
- 12 Ratte or other yellow-fleshed waxy potatoes
- 4 tablespoons (50 g) heavy cream
- 1 tablespoon chopped chives
- Lemon juice
- 1 ½ tablespoons (20 g) slightly salted butter
- Salt, freshly ground pepper

Wine suggestion: a white Alsace wine, such as Riesling grand cru Schoenenbourg, Deiss, 1993.

Sea Bass with Spider Crab Jus and Seafood Garnish

BY JEAN-FRANÇOIS PIÈGE

Soak the clams and razor clams for several hours in water with coarse salt added, away from the light.

Simmer the spider crab claws in *court-bouillon* for 3 minutes. Drain and shell, taking care not to break up the flesh. Clean the *supions* (small squid), wash and drain on a rack.

Cut the 3 garlic cloves into fine julienne and fry gently in the olive oil over a low heat for 15 minutes.

Cut the romaine lettuce leaves to the same size, then wash and dry. Peel the green onions and cook, covered, with a little olive oil for 10 minutes over a low heat.

Prepare the *jus*: make a vegetable stock with the carrot, onion, leek and fennel. Place the vegetables in a saucepan with the coconut, 3 crushed garlic cloves, coriander and the fennel sprig. Add just enough chicken stock to cover, bring to a boil, then cover and cook for 40 minutes. Add half the basil, remove from the heat and leave to infuse for 20 minutes.

Cut the spider crab shell into quarters. Reserve the coral. Sauté the shells over a high heat in a cast iron pot with a little olive oil. As soon as they begin to take color, add ½ stick (50 g) butter, and cook until the spider crab is lightly caramelized. Add 4 ounces (100 g) scallions, diagonally sliced, the chopped tomatoes, the rest of the crushed garlic and 1 lemon, cut into quarters. Simmer for a few minutes, then strain the vegetable stock over the spider crab and vegetables and simmer gently for 20 minutes. Add the rest of the basil, remove from the heat and leave to infuse for 20 minutes. Strain the entire contents

of the pot through a chinois (or fine sieve) and reduce slightly. Bind with 4 tablespoons (50 g) butter, a little olive oil and the coral, without letting it boil.

Soften 3 minced scallions in a large skillet with 4 tablespoons (50 g) butter. Add 1 crushed garlic clove and the *bouquet garni*. Add the drained clams and razor clams and the wine. Cover and cook over a high heat until the shells open, then add the spider crab stock. Remove the clams from their shells and remove the beards from the razor clams. Reduce the stock by half, add the crème fraîche, then return the clams and razor clams to the sauce, coating them with it. Peel one lemon and divide into segments, reserving the juice.

Briefly fry the *supions* in a skillet with a little olive oil. Drain, then slightly reduce the pan juices, and bind with ½ stick (50 g) butter, a little olive oil and a drop of lemon juice. Coat the *supions* in the sauce.

Soften the lemon segments for 2 minutes in a small pot with a little olive oil. Add the romaine lettuce, green onions and drained, cooked garlic. Simmer, uncovered, over a low heat for 1-2 minutes. Season with fine salt and pepper.

Brush the sea bass steaks with olive oil and season with salt. Place in a skillet and cook over a very low heat for 5 minutes on each side, without allowing them to take color.

Arrange all the ingredients on plates, adding a little *jus*. Serve the rest separately.

4 SERVINGS

- 4 sea bass steaks, each weighing 5 ½ ounces (160 g), cut from a 9-pound (4-kg) fish, skin and fat removed
- 12 clams, 4 razor clams
- 2 female spider crabs
- 1 pound (500 g) supions (small squid), court-bouillon
- 4 garlic cloves
- 10 Romaine lettuce leaves
- 12 green onions
- 3 scallions, minced
- 1 stick (100 g) unsalted butter
- 1 bouquet garni
- ½ cup (10 cl) white wine
- ¼ cup (50 g) crème fraîche
- 2 Menton lemons, coarse salt
- Fine sea salt

JUS

- 2 ounces (50 g) peeled carrot
- 4 ounces (100 g) each, white onion, leek and fennel, cut into pieces
- 1 pound (500 g) well-ripened tomatoes
- 4 ounces (100 g) shelled coconut
- 6 garlic cloves
- 10 coriander seeds
- 1 sprig wild or dried fennel
- 2 cups (50 cl) light chicken stock (see page 130)
- 1 bunch basil
- 1 stick (100 g) unsalted butter
- 4 ounces (100 g) peeled scallions

Wine suggestion: a white wine from the Rhône Valley, such as Hermitage "Chevalier de Sterimberg", Paul Jaboulet, 1989.

Sea Bass and Bacon Tournedos Meunière, with Green Lentils and Crispy Bacon

BY SYLVAIN PORTAY

Remove all the bones from the fish. Place the fish on a dish, cover with coarse salt and leave to rest for 1 hour.

Peel the baby onions, place them in a saucepan with 1 tablespoon (10 g) butter, 1 pinch salt, 2 pinches sugar and 4 tablespoons water. Cook until all the liquid has evaporated and turn the onions in the brown glaze that has formed in the pan. Cook the carrots in the same way.

Prepare the lentils: peel the onion and carrot, place them in a saucepan with the lentils, marrow bone and veal *jus*. Add enough water to cover. Season, cover, add the *bouquet garni* and cook for 35 minutes.

Rinse the fish under cold running water to remove the excess salt and dry thoroughly. Cut into 8 even slices 1 ¼ inches (3 cm) thick. Sandwich a rasher of bacon between two slices, shape into a round tournedos and tie with kitchen twine, with the skin side outwards. Make all 4 tournedos in the same way.

Preheat the oven to 400°F (200°C; gas mark 6). Season the tournedos with *mignonette* (coarsely ground white) pepper.

Melt 2 tablespoons (30 g) butter in a skillet. When the butter froths, brown the tournedos for 2-3 minutes on each side, then transfer them to the oven for 6-8 minutes.

Coarsely chop the parsley leaves. Peel and finely mince the scallion. Drain the lentils, reserving the stock.

Remove the tournedos from the oven and place them on a rack. Place 4 rashers of bacon between two baking sheets and bake in the oven for 5 minutes until crisp. Deglaze tournedos pan with cognac. Add the lentil stock and reduce by half. Check the seasoning then add 2 tablespoons (30 g) butter and ⅓ cup (10 cl) olive oil.

Place the lentils, onions and carrots in a skillet with 3 tablespoons of the reduced lentil stock. Bring to a boil, check the seasoning and bind with 1 ½ tablespoons (20 g) butter. Add the scallion and parsley and a drop of vinegar.

Arrange 2 tablespoons of lentils in the center of each warmed plate. Place one tournedos on each bed of lentils and top with 1 rasher of bacon. Cover with sauce and serve immediately.

4 SERVINGS

- 1 ½ pound (640 g) sea bass fillet, skinned
- 7 ounces (200 g) coarse salt
- 12 baby onions
- 1 stick (100 g) unsalted butter
- 4 ounces (120 g) carrots, cut into 1 ¼-inch (3-cm) dice
- 8 very thin rashers smoked streaky bacon
- ½ ounce (10 g) mignonette (coarsely ground white) pepper
- 2 sprigs parsley
- 1 scallion
- 4 tablespoons (5 cl) cognac
- ⅓ cup (10 cl) olive oil
- 1 drop sherry vinegar
- Sugar
- Salt, freshly ground pepper

LENTILS

- 1 onion
- 1 carrot
- 5 ounces (150 g) green lentils
- 1 marrow bone
- 1 scant cup (20 cl) veal jus (see page 130)
- 1 bouquet garni

Wine suggestion: a red wine from Provence, such as Bandol, Château de Pibarnon, 1989.

Sea Bass with Mediterranean Vegetable Salsa and Bouillabaisse Sauce

BY ALESSANDRO STRATTA

Prepare a tomato confit: preheat the oven on its very lowest setting. Plunge the tomatoes in boiling water for a few seconds, then pass them immediately under cold, running water. Peel, cut into quarters and deseed. Arrange the tomatoes on a baking sheet or ovenproof dish. Drizzle lightly with olive oil. Peel and crush the garlic clove and sprinkle over the tomatoes. Tear off the thyme leaves and sprinkle them over the tomatoes. Roast in the oven for 2 hours.

Prepare the bouillabaisse sauce: peel and mince the onion. Dice the leek and fennel. Peel and mince the garlic. Heat 2 tablespoons olive oil in a skillet over a high heat. Fry the onion, leek, fennel and garlic until golden. Add the saffron, crumbled thyme and dried fennel. Add the wine, scraping the base of the pan with a spatula, and cook until the wine has completely evaporated. Add the fish stock and reduce by two thirds. Add the rest of the oil in a steady stream, while stirring to create a smooth emulsion. Season and leave to stand at room temperature.

Prepare the vegetable salsa: soak the raisins in the vinegar. Dice the onion, zucchini and eggplant and lightly brown each vegetable separately in a nonstick skillet. Mix the vegetables with the minced garlic, raisins, pine nuts, capers, shredded basil and coarsely chopped parsley.

Season the sea bass fillets. Make diagonal incisions at regular intervals along the skin side. Seal the fish, skin side downwards for 5 minutes over a medium heat in a nonstick skillet with 1 tablespoon olive oil. Cook for 1 minute on the other side.

Deep fry the parsley leaves at 350°F (180°C). Briefly fry the vegetable salsa in a little olive oil over a very high heat. Divide the salsa between the 4 plates and arrange the fish on top. Garnish each plate with 2 pieces of tomato confit and fried parsley. Surround with bouillabaisse sauce. Serve immediately.

4 SERVINGS

- 4 sea bass fillets, each weighing
  6 ounces (175 g), cut from a
  6 ½-pound (3-kg) fish
- 2 tomatoes, olive oil
- 1 small garlic clove
- 1 small sprig thyme
- 4 sprigs parsley
- Salt, fresh ground pepper

BOUILLABAISSE SAUCE

- 1 cup (25 cl) virgin olive oil
- 1 small white onion
- ½ the white portion of a leek
- 3 ounces (80 g) fennel bulb
- 3 garlic cloves
- 1 teaspoon saffron threads,
  3 sprigs thyme
- 6 sprigs dried fennel
- 1 cup (25 cl) white wine
- 1 cup (25 cl) fish stock

MEDITERRANEAN VEGETABLE
SALSA

- 2 tablespoons raisins
- 2 tablespoons wine vinegar
- ½ cup (80 g) diced onion
- ½ cup (80 g) diced zucchini
- ½ cup (80 g) diced eggplant
- 2 tablespoons pine nuts
- 3 garlic cloves
- 1 tablespoon each, capers, basil
  and parsley

*Wine suggestion: a Provençal
white, such as Cassis Clos Sainte-
Madeleine.*

Breton Turbot with Shellfish

BY ALAIN DUCASSE

4 SERVINGS

FROM THE MARKET
- **1 turbot, weighing 18-20 pounds (8-9 kg)**
- **Olive oil**
- **2 tablespoons (30 g) unsalted butter**
- **Fine salt**

Sauce and garnish
- **40 cockles**
- **40 clams**
- **8 razor clams**
- **7 ounces (200 g) winkles**
- **2 Gilardeau (Marennes d'Oléron) oysters**
- **2 pounds (1 kg) mussels**
- **4 scallions**
- **1 ¼ sticks (120 g) unsalted butter**
- **1 ½ cups (40 cl) white wine**
- **2 cups (50 cl) light cream**
- **Salt**

Place the cockles, clams, razor clams and winkles in a large bowl of cold water with plenty of salt. Leave to soak for several hours away from the light.

Cut the turbot into 4 steaks, each weighing 1 pound (450 g), so providing 7 ounces (200 g) of flesh. Remove the skin from both sides by inserting a filleting knife with a long, flexible blade between flesh and skin.

Heat 1 tablespoon olive oil in a skillet. Add 2 tablespoons (30 g) butter. Seal the turbot steaks in the hot fat, then cook for 5-6 minutes on each side over a medium heat. Season with fine salt and baste frequently with the pan juices. The fish steaks should be lightly colored.

Prepare the sauce: peel and mince the scallions. Scrape the mussels and remove the beards. Wash in plenty of water. Discard any that remain open. Melt 1 ½ (20 g) tablespoons butter in a stew pot, add a quarter of the minced scallions and soften over a low heat for 5 minutes. Add ½ cup (10 cl) white wine and the mussels, and cook over a high heat until they open, shaking the pot frequently. Tip the contents of the pot into a sieve, collect the liquor, strain it through a chinois (or fine sieve), and reserve. Reserve the mussels to use in another dish.

Cook the shellfish for the garnish: rinse in plenty of water. Cook each type of shellfish in turn in 1 ½ tablespoons (20 g) butter with 1 minced scallion and ½ cup (10 cl) white wine, making sure they do not dry out. Reserve 8 cockles, 8 clams and 4 razor clams in their shells. Remove the rest from their shells. Discard the pale part of the razor clams. Discard the liquor.

● Choose a good quality turbot, weighing 18-20 pounds (8-9 kg).

● Cut 4 steaks, each weighing 1 pound (450 g), from the turbot.

● Cook the steaks in butter and olive oil.

● Cook the mussels in a stew pot over a high heat, to open them.

Bring a saucepan of water to a boil, add salt then place the winkles in the water and cook for 5-8 minutes, according to size. Drain and remove from their shells with a toothpick.

Pour the cream into a saucepan and reduce to three quarters. Heat the mussel liquor but do not allow it to boil. Add the reduced cream and 2 raw oysters, and stir in 3 ½ tablespoons (40 g) butter. Pass the mixture through a chinois (or fine sieve).

Preheat the oven to 350°F (180°C; gas mark 4). Heat the sauce but do not allow it to boil. Place the shell fish in a saucepan with a little sauce and heat through gently over a low heat. Once again, do not allow them to boil.

Reheat the turbot steaks in the oven for 3-4 minutes, Arrange them on the plates, sprinkle with the shelled seafood, adding 2 cockles, 2 clams and 1 razor clam to each plate. Top with 1 tablespoon sauce. Serve the rest of the sauce separately.

Wine suggestion: a white wine from the Loire Valley, such a Pouilly-fumé "pur sang", Didier Dagueneaux, 1997.

● Add the reduced cream to the mussel liquor.

● Add 2 raw oysters and 3 ½ tablespoons (40 g) butter.

● Stir the sauce , then strain it through a chinois (or fine sieve).

● Serve the turbot with the shellfish. Coat with sauce.

66 Breton turbot are fished all along the coast. They are fairly relaxed fish that like the sandy seabed where they hunt by day, while at night they trap their prey in deep water. 99

CONTENTS

● Alain Ducasse ●
Breton Turbot with Shellfish

Alain Ducasse chooses a truly "Atlantic" garnish to bring out the best in Breton turbot. Shellfish and mussel liquor are enriched with oysters and crème fraîche to add the distinctive flavor of the sea, as well as an interplay of textures and a touch of richness to this most noble of fish. The turbot is prized for its firm flesh and this recipe calls for a large fish yielding good, thick steaks which, when baked in the oven in a cast iron pot, will remain soft and tender.

● Franck Cerutti ●
Spit-roasted Turbot Steaks with Lemon Salsa and Swiss Chard

Because the turbot is spit-roasted, this recipe calls for a rather smaller fish, producing smaller steaks. The density of the turbot flesh makes for an interesting contrast with the different degrees of crispness of the diced salsa ingredients – lemon, olives, capers and pine nuts. The flavor of the fish is heightened by the acidity of the lemon, tempered somewhat by the olive oil. The soft smooth texture of the accompanying Swiss chard ribs and leaves is enlivened by the crunchiness of the minuscule croûtons.

• Jean-Louis Nomicos •
Fillets of Turbot Studded with Lemon Confit, Clams, Artichokes and Samphire au naturel

The tender, steamed turbot is delicately perfumed by the lemon confit. The addition of the clams to the pot brings a salty, iodized flavor, reinforced further by the samphire. This recipe highlights the contrast in textures: the firmness of the turbot and clam meat and the blend of crispness and softness of the artichokes and samphire. The thin *jus* harmonizes the grassy tastes of artichoke and samphire with the sharpness of lemon and iodine.

• Sylvain Portay •
Turbot Steaks, Potatoes, Tomatoes, Onion and Basil Baked in an Earthenware Dish

This recipe is a variation on the classic Provençal vegetable *tian*, this time using turbot. In order to retain all their tenderness, the steaks should be taken from a smaller fish, and cut so that they are about as wide as they are thick, otherwise they may become too dry. Lemon, basil and fennel add a distinctly Mediterranean touch, perfectly suited to the turbot's delicate flavor.

• Jean-François Piège •
Breton Turbot with Champagne Sabayon Glaze, Asparagus and Crawfish

This is a modern interpretation of a great classic of French cuisine: the traditional pairing of turbot and crawfish. The turbot must be a large one, and the steaks should be left on the bone to ensure tenderness and flavor. Champagne is added to the sauce at the last minute, in order to retain its sparkle and counterbalance the richness of the *sabayon*, whose consistency recalls mousseline sauce, the perfect partner to asparagus. This is one of the reasons for their presence – the other being their sharp flavor.

• Alessandro Stratta •
Turbot with Braised Celery, Black Truffles, and Potato Purée

To exploit to the full the consistency and remarkable firmness of the turbot flesh, Alessandro Stratta prepares it in the simplest way possible. The fish is pan-fried, but comes surrounded by a whole spectrum of textures: smooth purée, crisp truffles and crunchy celery salad, as well as soft braised celery and crisp celery root chips. The classic match of truffle and celery appears here in several variations: hot, cold, and in the sauce, so multiplying the taste sensations.

Spit-roasted Turbot Steaks with Lemon Salsa and Swiss Chard

BY FRANCK CERUTTI

The day before, plunge the tomatoes into boiling water, peel, cut into quarters and deseed. Coat the tomatoes with olive oil, arrange them on a large, ovenproof dish, season with salt and pepper and sprinkle them with a pinch of powdered thyme. Heat the oven on its very lowest setting and leave the tomatoes to dry out for 3 hours.

When you are ready to cook, separate the Swiss chard leaves from the ribs. Cut the ribs into 2 ½-inch (6-cm) pieces, remove any strings and soak in water with lemon juice. Cut the leaves into strips 1 ¼ inches (3 cm) wide.

Peel the garlic. Brown the Swiss chard ribs and the whole garlic clove in a little olive oil and 1 ½ tablespoons butter. Stir well to coat the vegetables. Add enough chicken stock to cover and simmer gently until all the liquid has evaporated. Once again, add enough chicken stock to cover and repeat the process until the ribs are tender.

Prepare the lemon salsa. Scrub 1 lemon under running water, remove the zest without the pith, and cut lengthwise into thin strips. Plunge the lemon zest in boiling water, refresh immediately and drain. Peel the 2 lemons completely, reserving the juice. Carefully divide into segments removing the membrane.

Preheat the oven to 400°F (200°C; gas mark 6). Spread the pine nuts over a baking sheet and bake in the oven for 3-5 minutes. Cut each piece of dried tomato in half. Drain the capers and olives. Cut the bread into ¼-inch (0.5 cm) dice.

Spit-roast the turbot, or roast in the oven, if preferred. Cook for 10 minutes. Baste the fish frequently with a mixture of olive oil and butter. When the fish is cooked, transfer to a rack and leave to rest for 5 minutes. Remove the skin and fillet. Season with salt and pepper, then put the steaks back together again.

While the fish is cooking, heat 1 ½ tablespoons (20 g) butter in a skillet. When the butter turns brown, sauté all the salsa ingredients for 2-3 minutes. Add 2 tablespoons of the reserved lemon juice, scraping the base of the pan with a spatula. Transfer the salsa to a small skillet, add just enough olive oil to cover but not to "drown" the ingredients, and leave to "mature" over a very low heat.

Heat the olive oil in a skillet and brown the Swiss chard leaves over a high heat for 3-4 minutes. Mix the leaves and ribs together. Fry the croûtons in a skillet with 2 tablespoons (30 g) butter, until golden.

Arrange the Swiss chard on the plates and sprinkle with croûtons. Place the turbot steaks alongside and cover with lemon salsa.

4 SERVINGS

- 1 turbot, weighing 6 ½ kg) cut into steaks (on the bone) each weighing 11 ounces (300 g)
- 4 ripe tomatoes
- ½ cup (10 cl) extra-virgin Ligurian olive oil
- Powdered thyme
- 1 bunch tender Swiss chard, with ribs
- Lemon juice
- 1 garlic clove
- 1 stick (100 g) unsalted butter
- 2 cups (50 cl) light chicken stock (see page 130)
- Fine salt
- Freshly ground pepper

LEMON SALSA

- 2 Menton lemons
- 1 tablespoon pine nuts
- 1 tablespoon small capers
- 12 "cailletier" olives
- 4 ounces (100 g) crustless bread

Wine suggestion: a white AOC Côtes-de-Provence, such as Clos Saint-Joseph, M. Sass

Fillets of Turbot Studded with Lemon Confit, Clams, Artichokes and Samphire au naturel

BY JEAN-LOUIS NOMICOS

Scrub the lemons under running water and dry with a cloth. Dissolve the sugar in 1 quart (1 l) water over a low heat and bring to a boil. Add the lemons, turn the heat down, cover the saucepan with a rack and a cloth to prevent the lemons floating to the surface, and cook over a very low heat for 6 hours. Leave the lemons to cool in the syrup.

Soak the clams for 1 hour under running water.

Drain the lemon confit. Cut the zest into strips 1 ¼ inches (3 cm) long and ⅛ inch (3 mm) wide. Make 5 incisions in each turbot steak and insert a strip of lemon zest in each one.

Peel the artichoke stalks, trim the tips of the leaves, cut off the leaves at the base with a small, sharp knife and remove the chokes. Cut lengthwise into slices.

Sort the samphire heads, wash in cold water and plunge them into a saucepan of boiling water for 30 seconds. Drain and refresh in iced water to stop the cooking process and preserve their color.

Preheat the oven to 350°F (180°C; gas mark 4). Boil the white wine for a few minutes to allow the alcohol to evaporate. Mince the scallion half.

Melt the butter in an ovenproof pot. Arrange the turbot steaks and artichokes in the pot. Add the white wine, scallion and parsley sprigs. Heat for 3 minutes over a high heat, then transfer to the oven and cook for 5-6 minutes. Three-quarters of the way through the cooking time, add the clams and samphire. If necessary, add a little chicken stock from time to time.

Leave the turbot steaks to rest on a rack for at least 5 minutes. Remove all the garnish ingredients from the pot. Discard the parsley. Shell 16 clams. Strain the cooking juices through a chinois (or fine sieve). Season lightly with a little lemon juice. Return all the garnish ingredients to the pot with the juices and reheat.

Cover the turbot with aluminum foil and return to the oven for 1 minute. Arrange on the plates with the garnish. Drizzle with the cooking juices.

4 SERVINGS

- 4 turbot steaks, each weighing
  5 ounces (150 g), cut from the
  back of a 13-pound (6-kg) turbot
- 28 clams
- 4 Menton lemons
- 1 ½ cups (300 g) sugar
- 6 small, young, purple Provençal
  artichokes
- 2 ounces (50 g) samphire
- ½ cup (10 cl) white wine
- ½ scallion
- 1 stick slightly salted butter
- 2 sprigs flat-leaf parsley
- ½ cup (10 cl) light chicken stock
  (see page 130)
- Lemon juice
- Freshly ground pepper

*Wine suggestion: an elegant white
Burgundy, such as
Chablis grand cru "Les Clos",
Jean Dauvissat, 1994.*

Breton Turbot with Champagne Sabayon Glaze, Asparagus and Crawfish

BY JEAN-FRANÇOIS PIÈGE

Prepare the crawfish and their *jus*. Remove the heads from 12 crawfish. Fry the crawfish tails for 3 minutes in a cast iron pot with a little olive oil. Remove the pot from the heat and add 5 crushed garlic cloves and the parsley. Cover with a damp cloth and leave to infuse for 15 minutes.

Shell the crawfish tails. Cut the shells and the 4 remaining crawfish into even-sized cubes. Sauté for 3 minutes in a stew pot over a high heat. Add the fennel and scallion, both diced, 3 garlic cloves, diced tomatoes, *bouquet garni* and dried fennel. Cover and simmer over a low heat for 3 minutes. Add the cognac and white wine, scraping the base of the pot with a spatula, and cook until all the liquid has evaporated. Add just enough water to cover the ingredients, then cook, covered, for 30 minutes. Remove from the heat, add the basil and *mignonette* (coarsely ground white) pepper, and leave to infuse for 15 minutes. Strain by holding down the solid ingredients with a wooden spoon. Reduce slightly, season with truffle *jus*, 1 ½ tablespoons olive oil, fine salt and pepper. Turn the crawfish tails in the mixture.

Start preparing the champagne sauce. Simmer the turbot head and wattles with 4 tablespoons (50 g) clarified butter for 5 minutes in a covered pot to render up the juices. Add the carrot, sliced mushrooms, crushed garlic cloves, minced scallions and fennel. Add enough champagne to cover, replace the lid and simmer for 40 minutes.

Peel and wash the asparagus. Lightly brown the two types of asparagus separately with a little olive oil. Add just enough chicken stock to cover the vegetables. Do not cover the pan. Cook the *demoiselles* for 8 minutes and the *bourgeoises* for 12 minutes. Coat them in the pan juices. Arrange the asparagus in bundles, placing 2 *demoiselles* on top of 3 *bourgeoises* and cutting the bases of the spears diagonally. Spoon the pan juices over the asparagus.

Scrub the truffles under running water. Peel and cut into 20 small sticks, ⅛ inch (3 mm) wide and 2 inches (5 cm) long.

Remove the champagne sauce from the heat, add the parsley and pepper and infuse for 20 minutes. Strain through a chinois (or fine sieve).

Prepare the sabayon: whisk the egg yolks over a *bain-marie*, while gently pouring in 1 cup (20 cl) champagne. When the mixture is thick and foamy, add the rest of the hot clarified butter. Keep warm in the *bain-marie*.

Cook the turbot with 4 tablespoons (50 g) foaming butter for 5 minutes on each side. Add a quarter of the crawfish juices and continue to cook for a further 3 minutes. Remove the turbot, cover and leave to rest in a warm place.

Add the champagne sauce to the turbot cooking juices. Reduce the mixture slightly, strain through the chinois and whisk in the sabayon to bind it. Strain again and check the seasoning. Season lightly with a little lemon juice and 2 tablespoons champagne.

Skin the fish. Arrange the steaks on the plates and cover with a little sauce. Garnish with crawfish tails, asparagus and sticks of raw truffle. Serve the rest of the sauce separately.

4 SERVINGS

- 4 turbot steaks, each weighing 8 ounces (220 g), cut from a turbot weighing 18 pounds (8 kg)
- 12 green "bourgeoise" asparagus spears
- 8 green "demoiselle" asparagus spears
- 1 (25 cl) light chicken stock (see page 130)
- 1 ½ ounces (40 g) black truffles
- Olive oil, ½ stick butter
- Fine salt, freshly ground pepper

CRAWFISH JUS
- 16 large crawfish with red claws
- 8 garlic cloves, crushed
- ¼ bunch parsley
- 3 ounces (80 g) each fennel and scallion
- 4 ½ ounces (120 g) tomatoes
- 1 bouquet garni
- 1 sprig dried fennel
- 2 tablespoons cognac
- ½ cup (10 cl) white wine
- ½ bunch basil
- ½ teaspoon mignonette (coarsely ground white) pepper
- 2 tablespoons truffle jus

CHAMPAGNE SAUCE
- Head and wattles of the turbot
- 1 stick (100 g) clarified, unsalted butter (see page 171)
- ½ cup (60 g) diced carrot
- 4 ounces (100 g) cultivated mushrooms
- 3 garlic cloves, 4 ounces (100 g) scallions
- 1 sprig dried fennel
- ½ bottle dry champagne
- ¼ bunch parsley
- 2 teaspoons mignonette (coarsely ground white) pepper
- 4 egg yolks, lemon juice

Wine suggestion: a white wine from the Rhône Valley, such as Saint-Péray, Bernard Gripa. 1994.

Turbot Steaks, Potatoes, Tomatoes, Onion and Basil Baked in an Earthenware Dish

BY SYLVAIN PORTAY

Remove the white skin from the turbot steaks, using a filleting knife with a long, sharp, flexible blade.

Peel the potatoes, then cut first into cylinders and then into ¹⁄₁₆-inch (2-mm) slices. Peel the onions and slice them into rounds. Peel and core the tomatoes and cut into ⅛-inch (3 mm) slices. Season each vegetable separately with salt, pepper and a little olive oil.

Grease 4 individual terracotta dishes. Rinse and dry the lemon and cut from it 4 very thin slices. Layer the vegetables in the dishes, starting with a layer of potato, followed by a layer of onion, and a layer of tomato. Continue in the same order until all the vegetables have been used. Insert 3 basil leaves among the ingredients in each dish, and place a slice of lemon and a sprig of fennel in the center. Drizzle generously with olive oil.

Preheat the oven to 400°F (200°C; gas mark 6). Heat the chicken stock. Season the fish and brush with olive oil. Moisten the vegetables in each dish with stock. Bring to a boil on top of the oven. Place a turbot steak on top of each dish, black skin upwards. Top with knobs of butter and cook in the oven for 15-20 minutes.

Just before serving, remove the black skin from the fish. Drizzle a little olive oil over each dish, sprinkle with a little fine salt and *mignonette* (coarsely ground white) pepper. Serve piping hot in the terracotta dishes. This dish can also be cooked in the oven in one large gratin dish and then served on hot plates.

4 SERVINGS

- 4 turbot steaks, each weighing
  9 ounces (250 g)
- 8 new potatoes
- 4 young onions, each a little
  larger than an egg
- 4 tomatoes
- 4 tablespoons (5 cl) olive oil
- 1 unwaxed lemon
- 12 basil leaves
- 4 sprigs dried fennel
- 1 ¼ cups (30 cl) light chicken
  stock (see page 130)
- 10 tablespoons (120 g) unsalted
  butter
- Fine salt
- Mignonette (coarsely ground
  white) pepper
- Salt
- Freshly ground pepper

SPECIAL UTENSILS

- 4 individual terracotta dishes

*Wine suggestion: a white
Côte de Beaune, such as
Meursault-Perrières premier cru,
Jean-François Coche-Dury, 1990.*

Turbot with Braised Celery, Black Truffles, and Potato Purée

BY ALESSANDRO STRATTA

Peel the truffles and mince the parings. Slice the truffles and cut the slices into large sticks of even size. Coarsely chop the trimmings.

Prepare the celery salad: grate the ribs of half a celery heart on a mandolin to create a fine julienne. Place the celery in a bowl. Add the truffle parings, half the parsley, chives and 2 tablespoons of yellow leaves from the celery. Mix 2 tablespoons olive oil with 1 tablespoon lemon juice, salt and pepper. Refrigerate the salad and vinaigrette separately.

Prepare the truffle sauce: place 2 tablespoons truffle parings in a food processor, add ¾ cup (80 g) diced celery ribs, 4 tablespoons chicken stock and ½ cup (12 cl) olive oil. Blend, season with salt and pepper and blend in 1 teaspoon lemon juice. Refrigerate the sauce.

Prepare the potatoes: peel and wash, place in a saucepan of cold water, add coarse salt and simmer for 25 minutes.

Braise the celery: remove the strings from 4 ½ ounces (125 g) celery ribs. Cut into small julienne. Melt 3 tablespoons (40 g) butter in a saucepan. Add the celery and soften over a low heat for 5 minutes. Season with salt and pepper. Stir thoroughly to coat the celery in melted butter. Add 1 cup (25 cl) chicken stock, scraping the base of the pan with a spatula. Reduce the liquid to a syrupy consistency. Add the truffle *jus* and 4 tablespoons truffle julienne. Keep warm.

Cook the turbot: remove the black skin. Heat 1 tablespoon olive oil in a skillet. Season the fish. Seal in the hot oil for 3 minutes on each side. Remove the white skin.

Cut the celery root into 12 thin, round chips. Preheat a deep-fryer to 350°F (180°C). Fry the chips until golden, then drain on absorbent paper.

Drain the potatoes, mash with a fork, adding a little olive oil and 3 tablespoons (40 g) butter. Adjust the seasoning. Add the rest of the parsley.

Toss the celery salad in the vinaigrette. Arrange the potato purée and braised celery on the plates. Arrange the turbot steaks on the bed of potato and celery, topped with the celery salad. Garnish with truffle sauce, celery root chips and chervil sprigs.

4 SERVINGS

- 4 turbot steaks, each weighing 8 ounces (225 g)
- 4 ½ ounces (120 g) black truffles
- 2 firm celery hearts
- 4 tablespoons coarsely chopped flat-leaf parsley
- 1 tablespoon minced chives
- Virgin olive oil
- Lemon juice
- 1 ¼ cups (30 cl) light chicken stock (see page 130)
- 4 - 5 Charlotte potatoes
- 6 tablespoons (80 g) unsalted butter
- 2 tablespoons truffle juice
- ½ celery root
- 2 sprigs chervil
- Oil for deep frying
- Coarse salt
- Salt, freshly ground black pepper

Wine suggestion: a white Burgundy, such as Chablis grand cru "Les Clos", René et Vincent Dauvissat.

Spit-roasted Suckling Lamb, Seasonal Vegetables and Dried Fruit Condiment

BY ALAIN DUCASSE

4 SERVINGS

FROM THE MARKET
- 2 pounds (1 kg) suckling lamb, cut from the undressed fillet
- 1 orange
- 12 chestnuts
- Veal jus (see page 130)
- 1 sprig dried fennel
- 4 garlic cloves
- 4 small fennel bulbs
- Olive oil
- 1 ½ cups (40 cl) light chicken stock (see page 130)
- 12 small, purple Provençal artichokes
- Juice of ½ lemon
- 8 ounces (200 g) chanterelles
- 4 ounces (100 g) horn of plenty mushrooms
- 1 scallion
- 12 grapes
- 2 rougettes (small lettuce from the south of France with reddish leaves)

- Salt

Ask the butcher to remove the nerves and fat from the meat and to cut the fillet into 4 pieces, each weighing about 6 ounces (180 g).

Prepare the lamb *jus*: peel and slice the scallion and onions. Peel and crush the garlic clove. Place the cubed lamb in a stew pot with a little olive oil and brown over a high heat. Add the scallion, garlic and white onions. Cover and soften the vegetables over a low heat for 10 minutes. Skim off most of the fat with a ladle, then add enough water to half cover the ingredients. Cook, uncovered, until all the liquid has evaporated, then add enough water to cover, and simmer gently for 1 ½ hours. Strain through a chinois (or fine sieve) and refrigerate.

Scrub the orange under running water, pat dry, then peel off a strip of zest ¾ inch (1.5 cm) wide. Squeeze half the orange. Place the zest in a saucepan with 2 tablespoons orange juice, and ½ cup (12 cl) lamb *jus*. Reduce to syrupy consistency. Leave to cool, then brush the 4 portions of lamb with the orange glaze and refrigerate.

Plunge the chestnuts into a saucepan of boiling water. Leave for 1-2 minutes, then remove from the water one by one and peel, taking care to remove both layers of skin. Place the chestnuts in a small pot, with just enough veal *jus* to cover, and the sprig of dried fennel. Cook, covered, over a low heat for 40 minutes.

Place the whole, unpeeled garlic cloves in a small skillet with a little olive oil. Cover and roast over a low heat for 30 minutes.

Remove the bases and tough stalks from the fennel. Cut each bulb in half lengthwise, then in half again so that each bulb is divided into 4 quarters. Place in a saucepan with 1 tablespoon olive oil, cover and soften for 5 minutes over a low heat. Season the fennel and add 1 cup (20 cl) light chicken stock. Bring to a boil, cover and cook for 15 minutes, until very soft.

Remove any hard or withered leaves from the artichokes. Peel the stalks. Trim the leaves to two thirds of their length, then remove them with a small, sharp knife, peeling around the heart. Only keep the hearts. Remove the chokes. Place the artichoke hearts in water with a little lemon juice. Drain and place in a saucepan with 1 tablespoon olive oil, cover and soften for 5 minutes over a low heat. Season, then add 1 cup (20 cl) light chicken stock. Bring to a boil, cover and cook for about 15 minutes, until the artichoke hearts are tender, checking them by inserting the point of a knife.

Clean all the mushrooms, washing them quickly and wiping dry. Peel and finely mince the scallion. Heat 1 tablespoon olive oil in a skillet and soften the scallion in the hot oil for 2 minutes. Add the mushrooms, season with salt and sauté over a high heat for about 10 minutes.

Lamb jus
- 1 ½ pounds (600 g) neck or breast of lamb, cubed
- 1 gray scallion
- 2 white onions
- 1 garlic clove
- Olive oil

Dried fruit condiment
- 2 anchovy fillets, preserved in salt
- 10 sultanas
- 8 almonds (preferably fresh)
- 2 preserved or dried apricots
- 4 garlic cloves
- 3 tablespoons (40 g) unsalted butter
- 1 teaspoon sugar
- 2 slices white bread, cut into small dice
- Vinegar
- 1 sprig rosemary, minced
- 2 tablespoons dried breadcrumbs

● Trim the lamb fillet: remove the nerves and fat.

● Reduce the orange juice with orange zest and lamb *jus.*

● Brush the lamb portions with the orange syrup.

● Plunge the chestnuts in boiling water and peel them.

● Remove the hard base and stalks from the fennel bulbs and cut in half.

● Remove the tough outer leaves of the artichokes. Peel the stalks, working around the heart.

● Cook the artichokes with a tablespoon of olive oil for 5 minutes over a low heat.

● Sauté the mushrooms for 10 minutes over a high heat with a softened scallion.

Wash and peel the grapes and remove the seeds with the point of a knife or a toothpick. Separate the *rougette* leaves, select the 12 most attractively shaped leaves around the heart and trim them to a uniform shape.

Prepare the dried fruit condiment: rinse the anchovies under running water, then leave them to soak in a bowl of cold water. Soak the sultanas in a cup of lukewarm water to rehydrate them. If using fresh almonds, open them and slice in half. Cut the apricots into strips.

Peel, quarter and degerm the garlic cloves. Melt 2 tablespoons (20 g) butter in a small skillet, and lightly brown the garlic. Sprinkle with the sugar, continue to cook for 2 minutes, then remove the garlic from the skillet.

Cut off the bread crusts and cut the slices into small croûtons. Melt 1 tablespoon (10 g) butter in a skillet, fry the croûtons until golden, then drain on absorbent paper.

● Select the 12 most attractively shaped leaves around the heart and trim them to a uniform shape.

● Assemble the condiment ingredients.

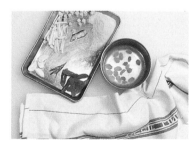

● Soak the sultanas in lukewarm water to rehydrate them.

● Cut the bread into small croûtons and fry in 1 tablespoon (10 g) butter, until golden.

Drain the sultanas. Melt 1 tablespoon (10 g) butter in a skillet. Lightly brown the almonds and sultanas in the hot butter, then add the croûtons and apricot strips. Add a few drops of vinegar and 1 tablespoon lamb *jus* and leave to caramelize.

Drain the anchovies and mash them with a fork. Mince the rosemary leaves. Sprinkle the contents of the skillet with breadcrumbs (to bind the condiment and add crunchy texture), then add the mashed anchovies and minced rosemary to flavor.

Spit-roast the lamb portions for 15 minutes. If you do not have a rôtisserie, brown the meat all round in a hot, ovenproof skillet, then roast in the oven at 400°F (200°C; gas mark 6) for 12 minutes. When the meat is cooked, leave it to rest on a rack for 10 minutes.

Place all the vegetables in a stew pot. Add the 12 *rougette* leaves, garlic confit and grapes. Bind with ½ cup (10 cl) lamb *jus*. Heat through gently over a low heat while the meat is resting.

Arrange a portion of lamb in the center of each plate, surround with vegetables and top each portion of meat with a tablespoon of dried fruit condiment. Serve the remaining condiment separately.

Wine suggestion: a red wine from Provence, such as AOC Les Baux-de-Provence, Clos Milan, 1995.

● Rinse the anchovies. Dry on absorbent paper and mash them with a fork.

● Lightly brown the almonds and sultanas, then add the croûtons and the apricot strips.

● Bind the vegetables, garlic confit and *rougette* in a skillet with ½ cup (10 cl) lamb *jus*.

● Top each portion of lamb with a tablespoon of the condiment and surround with vegetables.

" Slaughtered at the age of 45 days, the lamb will only have been fed on its mother's milk: a genuine suckling lamb. The meat is extremely tender and is a delicate shade of pink. "

CONTENTS

● Alain Ducasse ●
Spit-roasted Suckling Lamb, Seasonal Vegetables and Dried Fruit Condiment

A complex array of tasty ingredients, each in its own right a classic accompaniment to lamb, brings out the best in the simply spit-roasted meat. Alain Ducasse follows the Italian tradition through his use of rosemary and that of Provence through the addition of garlic. The dish also includes anchovies, featured in many ancient recipes, and dried fruit to add a Moroccan touch. Meanwhile, the vegetable garnish offers milder flavors, concentrating more on texture, with the discreet bite of the artichokes and lettuce, the softness of the chestnuts, the juiciness of the grapes, the firmness of the mushrooms and the richness of the garlic confit.

● Franck Cerutti ●
Roast Lamb with Parmesan Fennel, Green Onions and Baby Fava Beans Sautéed with Savory

Suckling lamb, green onions and baby fava beans give this dish a distinctly spring-like feel. The meat is plain roasted — on no account should it be pink — and classically highlighted by the fragrant savory. Equally classic is the use of fennel, served here with a simple sprinkling of Parmesan. Its subtle anise flavor is a delicious complement to the lamb.

• Jean-Louis Nomicos •
Rack of Lamb with Spiced
Souris and Sweetbreads

While the rack of lamb is roasted *"au naturel"*, the *souris* (or knuckle ends) are seasoned with a sophisticated, very Moroccan, collection of flavors – apricots, cumin, cinnamon, lemon and the North African spice mix known as *ras el hanout*. The Moroccan theme continues with the addition of almonds to the *jus*. Pepper and ginger add piquancy to the sweetbread coating. The semolina garnish recalls *panisse*, the chick pea or cornmeal cake typical of Nice and Marseilles.

• Sylvain Portay •
Roast Fillet of Lamb with Glazed Lamb
Ribs, Potatoes Roasted with Bacon,
Tomato Confit and Green Onions

In this recipe, Sylvain Portay offers distinctive contrasts, between the two ways of preparing the meat, and between the two different garnishes. The lamb is roasted in the traditional manner, while the ribs are boiled and grilled to produce American-style spare ribs with a version of Bar-B-Q sauce. The tender meat of the fillet contrasts with the crisply caramelized ribs. The potatoes embellished with onions and smoked bacon strike a northern note, while the tomato confit and green onions evoke the south.

• Jean-François Piège •
Roast Pyrenean Suckling Lamb with
Lamb's Liver Ragout and Red Pepper

The whole idea of this dish is to use every part of the suckling lamb, with its very delicate flavor and its rather limp texture. By contrast, the ragout of liver and other variety meats provides denser texture and stronger flavor. Pyrenean lamb is chosen for its consistent quality. It is seasoned with by *piment d'Espelette*, a hot pepper which, like the lamb itself, hails from the Basque Country. Whole peppers also feature as a garnish, stuffed with potatoes mashed with olive oil in the style of a *brandade*.

• Alessandro Stratta •
Rack of Lamb in a Herb Crust,
Pepper Ragout and Socca Niçoise

In this fairly simple but very Mediterranean recipe, the lamb is coated with a herb crust, lending the meat all the fragrance of the garden and the southern French countryside. The sweetness and piquancy of the mixed pepper ragout contrasts with the strongly flavored tapenade, while the *socca* provides the inimitable taste of chick pea flour. Delightfully encapsulating the spirit of the Nice region, the dish is enhanced by an interplay of textures, ranging from slightly gritty, through crunchy, to soft and smooth.

Roast Lamb with Parmesan-seasoned Fennel, Green Onions and Baby Fava Beans Sautéed with Savory

BY FRANCK CERUTTI

Rub the meat all over with savory. Spike the kidneys with savory.

Remove the hard base and stalks of the fennel bulbs. Cut each bulb in half and remove the bulging outer layers. Bring a saucepan of water to a boil, add salt, then cook the fennel for 15 minutes. Check with the point of a knife and drain.

Shell 1 pound (500 g) baby fava beans. Peel the green onions and the 4 garlic cloves.

Preheat the oven to 400°F (200°C; gas mark 6). Lightly season the chopped neck of lamb with salt. Heat 2 tablespoons olive oil in a large roasting pan. Add 2 tablespoons (30 g) butter. Brown the meat in the hot fat.
Add the shank or shanks of lamb and the kidneys. Baste with the fat, then place in the oven and cook for 10 minutes. Add the saddle of lamb, baste with the oil and butter and return the pan to the oven. Add the rack 10 minutes later. Baste with the hot fat (adding more if necessary) and cook for a further 10 minutes. Suckling lamb should be medium done.

Add the green onions and garlic 5 minutes before the end of the cooking time. If the lamb is very small, reduce each period of cooking time by 3-4 minutes. If preparing only 2 shanks, cook for 30 minutes.

Place the meat on a rack. Reserve the green onions and garlic separately. Skim off half the fat from the pan juices. Deglaze with a little light chicken stock, scraping the base of the pan with a spatula. Repeat the deglazing process three more times, then tip all the contents of the pan into a skillet and reduce for 20 minutes. Strain the pan juices. Add the green onions and garlic and a pinch of savory. Remove from the heat and leave to infuse for 10-15 minutes.

Heat 1 tablespoon olive oil in a skillet and add 1 ½ tablespoons (20 g) butter. Brown the fennel and sprinkle it with Parmesan cheese.

Heat 1 tablespoon olive oil in a skillet and fry the baby fava beans with a little savory for a few minutes until they burst. Season with salt.

Reheat the sauce and add the juices given off by the meat. Arrange the meat and vegetables on the plates. Add a little sauce and serve immediately.

4 SERVINGS

- 2 shanks of suckling lamb, or 1 shank, 1 saddle and 2 racks
- 4 lamb's kidneys, with most of their fat
- 1 neck of suckling lamb, chopped
- 1 bunch savory
- 4 large fennel bulbs
- 1 pound (500 g) baby fava beans
- 8 green onions
- 4 green garlic cloves
- Olive oil
- ½ stick (50 g) unsalted butter
- 1 cup (25 cl) light chicken stock (see page 130)
- ½ cup (50 g) grated Parmesan cheese
- Coarse salt
- Fine salt
- Freshly ground pepper

Wine suggestion: a red wine from Provence, such as AOC Bellet, Cuvée "Baron G", G. de Charnacé.

Rack of Lamb with Spiced Souris and Sweetbreads

BY JEAN-LOUIS NOMICOS

Preheat the oven to 325°F (160°; gas mark 3). Place 1 tablespoon olive oil and 1 ½ tablespoons (20 g) butter in a stew pot with the lamb *souris* (the small, rounded piece of meat at the knuckle end of the shank). Cover and cook over a low heat for 10 minutes. Add the peeled and crushed garlic cloves, the peeled and sliced white onions, the peeled and sliced apple, dried apricots, ½ vanilla pod, *ras el hanout* (North African spice mix), cinnamon, lemon zest, and 1 pinch each Cayenne pepper and cumin. Stir thoroughly, then cook, covered for 5 minutes. Add enough lamb *jus* to cover, then transfer to the oven and cook, covered, for 2 hours, until the *souris* are very soft and tender. Remove the *souris* from the pot and strain the cooking juices through a chinois (or fine sieve). Reduce by half and check the seasoning.

Prepare the semolina slices: bring the milk to a boil with 2 tablespoons (25 g) butter, salt, pepper and a pinch of nutmeg. Add the semolina and stir briskly for 15 minutes. Remove from the heat and stir in the grated Parmesan, egg yolks and 1 tablespoon heavy cream. Spread the mixture on a buttered dish in a layer about ¾ inch (1.5 cm) thick and leave to cool.

Rub the racks of lamb with crushed black pepper and fine salt. Cook under the grill for 15 minutes, exposing the fat to the heat source as much as possible.

Prepare the spiced honey: crush the pepper and coriander seeds. Mix all the spices with ½ teaspoon honey. Season the lamb's sweetbreads with salt and pepper and coat lightly with flour. Roll the sweetbreads in the spiced honey. Heat 1 ½ tablespoons (20 g) butter in a skillet until it foams. Cook the sweetbreads in the butter for a few minutes, turning frequently.

Leave the racks of lamb and sweetbreads to rest on a rack for 5 minutes.

Heat the oil in a deep-fryer to a temperature of 350°F (180°C). Cut the semolina into diamonds or small sticks 1 ½ inches (3.5 cm) long. Coat first in beaten egg and then in white breadcrumbs mixed with crushed hazelnuts. Deep fry until golden and drain on absorbent paper.

Cut the lamb *souris* in half. Reheat them in their cooking juices. Cut the peeled almonds into slivers and add to the juices.

Spoon a little juice onto each place. Cut the racks of lamb in two and arrange on the plates with the *souris*, sweetbreads and the semolina slices. Serve piping hot.

4 SERVINGS

- 2 racks of suckling lamb, each consisting of 6 ribs
- 4 souris of lamb
- 7 ounces (200 g) lamb's sweetbreads
- Olive oil, 3 tablespoons (40 g) unsalted butter
- 3 garlic cloves
- 4 ounces (100 g) white onions
- 1 Granny Smith apple
- 4 dried apricots
- ½ vanilla pod
- ½ teaspoon ras el hanout (North African spice mix, available from Middle Eastern food stores)
- 1 small piece cinnamon stick
- 2 pinches grated lemon zest
- Cayenne pepper, cumin
- 2 cups (50 cl) lamb jus (see page 208)
- Crushed black pepper, fine salt
- Oil for deep frying
- ¾ ounce (20 g) fresh almonds

SPICED HONEY

- Chestnut blossom honey
- 1 heaped teaspoon (2 g) each, ground coriander, ginger, cinnamon and mace
- 10 Sarawak (Malaysian) peppercorns
- 10 coriander seeds

SEMOLINA SLICES

- 1 cup milk, 2 tablespoons unsalted butter
- ⅓ cup (60 g) fine semolina
- ¼ cup (25 g) grated Parmesan cheese, heavy cream
- 2 egg yolks plus 1 whole egg
- Salt, pepper, nutmeg
- ⅓ cup (50 g) dried breadcrumbs
- ⅛ cup (20 g) toasted hazelnuts

Wine suggestion: a young, fruity Alsace wine, such as Pinot Noir Beaune, premier cru. "Clos-du-Roi". M. Toillot-Beaut. 1996.

Roast Pyrenean Suckling Lamb with Lamb's Liver Ragout and Red Pepper

BY JEAN-FRANÇOIS PIÈGE

Prepare the lamb *jus*: heat the oil in a cast iron pot, brown the meat, remove some of the fat, then add the diagonally sliced scallions, crushed garlic and savory. Cover and soften the vegetables for 5 minutes over a low heat. Add a ladleful of light chicken stock, scraping the base of the pot with a spatula. Add just enough stock to cover, simmer until all the liquid has evaporated, then add the rest of the stock and reduce to a syrup. Strain through a chinois (or fine sieve) and check the seasoning.

Prepare the liver ragout: remove the skin surrounding the liver and cut into 4 large strips. Remove the skin and fat surrounding the heart and cut into 4 large pieces. Remove the fat from the kidneys and cut each kidney in half. Remove the membrane covering the sweetbreads. Soak the brains under running water. Cut one brain into quarters and mince the other.

Prepare the garnish: cook the peppers on a griddle or under the grill until the skin turns black. Peel, core and deseed the peppers, but leave them whole. Place them in a bowl, cover with olive oil and leave to marinate. *Piquillo* peppers are long, slender red peppers from Spain - the name translates as "little birds' beaks". They have a very thin skin and piquant flavor.

Wash the potatoes, place them in a saucepan of cold water, bring to a boil and cook for 20 minutes. Peel the potatoes while still hot and mash them with a fork. Blend in the olive oil and season with salt and pepper. Rinse and dry the parsley. Tear off the leaves and add them to the mashed potatoes.

Fillet the lamb leaving the *panoufle* (the layer of skin and muscle) attached to the meat. Remove the nerves and excess fat. Roll the *panoufle* around the fillet and secure with kitchen twine. Fry the meat in a skillet over a high heat until the skin is crisp. Turn down the heat and add the crushed garlic and savory. Cook for 10-12 minutes, then keep warm for 10 minutes.

Heat a little olive oil in a cast iron skillet. Brown the liver, heart, kidneys, sweetbreads and the cut pieces of brain over a high heat for 3 minutes. Pour off the fat and add the red wine, scraping the base of the pan with a spatula. Add 2 tablespoons lamb *jus* and bind with the minced brain. Coat the ingredients in the sauce and check the seasoning. Season with *piment d'Espelette* (or cayenne pepper) and savory heads. Remove from the heat.

Drain the peppers and fill them with mashed potatoes. Untie the meat. Remove the *panoufle* and cut off all the fat, leaving only the crisp skin. Check the seasoning. Cut each fillet in two and cut the skin into similar sized pieces.

Divide the ragout between the four plates. Add the fillet of lamb and crisp skin, with the stuffed pepper on the side. Surround with a little lamb *jus* and serve piping hot.

4 SERVINGS

- ½ rack of Pyrenean suckling lamb
- 2 garlic cloves, crushed
- 1 sprig savory
- Fine salt, freshly ground pepper

LIVER RAGOUT

- 1 liver, 1 heart, 2 kidneys, 4 sweetbreads, 2 brains, all from suckling lambs
- Olive oil, 1 garlic clove
- ½ cup (10 cl) red wine
- Ground piment d'Espelette (or cayenne pepper)
- 10 savory heads

LAMB JUS

- 4 pounds (2 kg) neck or breast of lamb, cut into small pieces
- Generous ½ cup (15 cl) grapeseed oil
- 4 ounces (100 g) scallions, 1 head garlic
- 1 sprig savory
- 2 quarts (2 l) light chicken stock (see page 130)

GARNISH

- 4 red "piquillo" peppers
- 1 pound (500 g) Ratte or other yellow-fleshed waxy potatoes
- 1 ¼ cups (30 cl) olive oil
- ½ bunch flat-leaf parsley

Wine suggestion: a red wine from the Rhône Valley, such as Gigondas, cuvée de la Tour Sarrazine, M. Archimbaud, 1991.

Roast Fillet of Lamb with Glazed Lamb Ribs, Potatoes Roasted with Bacon, Tomato confit and Green Onions

BY SYLVAIN PORTAY

Prepare the onion and pepper glaze: wash the peppers, remove the core and the base, cut down one side and open them out. Remove the white ribs and seeds. Arrange the peppers on a baking sheet, skin side upwards, and place under the grill. When the skins begin to blacken, transfer to a salad bowl and cover with saran wrap. Leave to stand for a few minutes, then remove the skins while still hot. Rinse and drain in a colander.

Peel the onions and cut them into rings. Place them in a skillet with the olive oil, ½ head of unpeeled garlic, salt, pepper and *bouquet garni*. When they begin to produce water, cover with baking parchment. Cook until all the liquid has evaporated; the onions should be thoroughly cooked and translucent. Strain through a colander to remove excess oil. Discard the *bouquet garni* and garlic.

Process the peppers and onions separately in a blender, then place them together over a low heat to dry out. Add the honey, tomato ketchup and a few drops of Tabasco. Check the seasoning and leave to cool.

Prepare the racks of lamb. Preheat the oven to 400°F (200°C; gas mark 6). Detach the "eyes" of the rib chops, cutting along the ribs. Remove the nerve and fat. Reserve the fillets. Cook the ribs for 20 minutes in boiling water with a pinch of coarse salt, then refresh and drain. Spread the onion and pepper glaze over the meaty part of the ribs and cook in the oven for 10 minutes.

Prepare the potatoes: peel the potatoes and cut them into ¾-inch (2-cm) slices. Trim them to create neat rounds and place them in a bowl of water. Peel and dice the onion. Cut the bacon into large squares and brown in an ovenproof skillet. When the bacon begins to render up its fat, add the onion. Cook over a low heat, stirring from time to time, until well browned.

Dry the potatoes carefully and season them. Cook in ½ cup (10 cl) very hot oil until golden on both sides. Add 2 tablespoons (30 g) butter. Add veal stock so that the potatoes are three-quarters covered. Cover the potatoes with onion and bacon and bring to a boil. Transfer to the oven and cook for 25 minutes.

Cook the lamb fillets in the oven for 10 minutes at 400°F (200°C; gas mark 6), then leave to rest on a rack.

Peel the green onions and sauté in 1 tablespoon olive oil. Add a few tablespoons of light chicken stock and continue to cook until tender. Add the pieces of tomato confit and heat through gently.

Reheat the lamb *jus*. Cut the ribs into pairs and reheat them in the oven.

Ensure that the plates are very hot and place two rounds of potato in the center of each one. Arrange 2 pairs of ribs on top and surround with tomatoes and green onions. Slice the fillets in half then slice in half again diagonally. Place two slices of fillet on either side of each plate. Coat with sauce and serve immediately.

4 SERVINGS

- 2 racks of lamb, with bone, each consisting of 8 rib chops
- 4 green onions
- Light chicken stock (see page 130)
- 8 pieces tomato confit (see page 93)
- 1 cup (20 cl) lamb jus (see page 208)
- Salt and pepper, coarse salt

ONION AND PEPPER GLAZE
- 4 sweet peppers
- 2 large onions
- ½ cup (10cl) olive oil
- ½ head garlic
- 1 bouquet garni
- 1 teaspoon honey
- 1 teaspoon tomato ketchup
- Tabasco

POTATOES WITH BACON
- 2 pounds (1 kg) new potatoes
- 1 onion
- 3 rashers streaky bacon
- ½ cup (10 cl) olive oil
- 2 tablespoons (30 g) unsalted butter
- Veal stock (adapted from recipe for light chicken stock, page 130)

Wine suggestion: a red wine from south-western France, such as Madiran, Château Montus, 1989.

Rack of Lamb in a Herb Crust, Pepper Ragout and Socca Niçoise

BY ALESSANDRO STRATTA

Prepare the *socca niçoise* batter. Place the flour in a bowl. Add 1 ½ cups (37 cl) water in a steady stream and stir to create a smooth batter. Add 2 tablespoons olive oil and season with salt and pepper. Strain through a sieve and leave the batter to rest in the refrigerator for 2 hours.

Prepare the herb butter: rinse the parsley, pat dry, tear off the leaves and chop them coarsely. Peel, degerm and crush the garlic cloves. Place the garlic, parsley, chives, rosemary, sage, savory, thyme, butter, breadcrumbs, salt and pepper in a blender. Process to a smooth paste and refrigerate.

Make the tapenade: rinse the anchovy fillet and pat dry. Place the olives, anchovy, basil, vinegar and ½-¾ cup (12-18 cl) olive oil in a blender. Process until the mixture is still quite firm and slightly lumpy. Season with pepper. Reserve at room temperature.

Prepare the pepper ragout: arrange the sweet and hot peppers and onion on a baking sheet. Wrap the garlic in aluminum foil and add it to the other vegetables. Slide the baking sheet under the grill, or broil on the barbecue, until the skins begin to blacken. Cover the vegetables with saran wrap and leave to stand for 10 minutes.

Preheat the oven to 300°F (150°C; gas mark 2). Remove the skin, core, seeds and white ribs from all the peppers. Peel the onion. Cut the peppers and onions into strips. Peel the garlic and cut the cloves into pieces.

Heat the olive oil in a stew pot and cook the vegetables over a medium heat. Add the honey and season with salt and pepper. Transfer to the oven and cook until all the pan juices have evaporated. Remove from the oven and reserve at room temperature.

Cook the meat. Increase the oven temperature to 450°F (230°C; gas mark 8). Season the rack of lamb. Heat a little olive oil in a roasting pan. Seal on the lean side for 3 minutes. Transfer to the oven and cook for 8-9 minutes. Spread the herb butter over the meat. Slide the pan under the grill and leave until the butter forms a golden crust. Remove from the heat and leave to rest for 5 minutes.

Prepare the *socca*. Lightly brush a small, nonstick skillet with olive oil. Add a ladleful of batter. Cook for about 1 minute on each side. Transfer the *socca* to a hot dish, and cook the required number of portions.

Divide the pepper ragout between the 4 plates, with the lamb and tapenade alongside. The dish can be garnished with fried parsley. Serve the *socca* on the plates or separately.

4 SERVINGS

- 2 racks of lamb, each weighing
  1 pound (500 g)
- 1 bunch flat-leaf parsley
- 4 tablespoons chives
- 2 tablespoons each rosemary,
  sage, savory and thyme
- 6 garlic cloves
- 2 sticks (200 g) softened,
  unsalted butter
- 5 tablespoons dried breadcrumbs
- Salt, pepper, olive oil

TAPENADE

- ¾ cup (125 g) black olives, pitted
- 1 anchovy fillet, preserved in salt
- 2 tablespoons basil
- 1 teaspoon sherry vinegar
- ¾ cup (18 cl) olive oil

PEPPER RAGOUT

- 1 red, 1 yellow, 1 green pepper
- 2 fresh hot red peppers
- 1 red onion, 8 garlic cloves
- 2 tablespoons olive oil
- 2 tablespoons lavender honey

SOCCA NIÇOISE

- ¾ cup (125 g) chick pea flour
- 4 tablespoons olive oil

*Wine suggestion: A Spanish red,
such as Ribera del Duero
"Janus", Desquera.*

Candied Menton Lemons, Filled with Fresh Basil Sorbet, and Glazed Grapefruit Tartlets

BY ALAIN DUCASSE

4 SERVINGS

FROM THE MARKET
- 4 Menton lemons, with leaves
- 2 pounds (1 kg) superfine sugar
- 1 pink Florida grapefruit
- ½ cup (55 g) glucose (available from pharmacies)
- 1 sprig basil, plus 8 leaves
- 1 tablespoon flour
- 3 tablespoons (40 g) unsalted butter

Dough
- 1 ¾ cups (250 g) flour
- 1 ½ sticks (150 g) unsalted butter
- Generous ¼ cup (65 g) sugar
- 1 egg
- 1 lemon

Prepare the lemons three or four days in advance. Scrub the lemons under warm, running water and pat dry. Cut off both ends of each lemon. Scrape out all the lemon pulp, using a spoon with a serrated edge or a grapefruit knife.

Store the pulp in the refrigerator for making the sorbet. Place the empty lemon shells, cut-off ends and lemon leaves in a saucepan. Cover with plenty of cold water and bring to a boil. Boil for 2 minutes, then drain. Refresh immediately under cold, running water.

Prepare the candied lemons: place shells, ends and leaves in a saucepan with ½ cup (100 g) sugar and 2 cups (50 cl) water. Heat over a low heat. When the syrup reaches boiling point, turn off the heat and leave to stand.

The following day, add ½ cup (100 g) sugar to the saucepan containing the fruit and reheat over a low heat. When the syrup comes to a boil, turn off the heat and leave to stand. Repeat the process for one or two days more, adding ½ cup (100 g) sugar each time.

The day before the meal, prepare the dough: scrub the lemon under warm, running water, pat dry and finely grate the zest. Quickly mix the flour with the diced butter, egg and lemon zest to create a smooth dough. Roll into a ball, encase in saran wrap and leave to rest in the refrigerator.

The orange wine can also be prepared several days ahead. Scrub the oranges under warm, running water and pat dry. Cut the oranges into quarters or slices and cut the half lemon in the same way.

Pour the fruit spirit into a saucepan and add the sugar, rosé wine, oranges, lemon and vanilla. Bring to a boil, then remove the pan from the heat and leave to cool. Strain the orange wine and store in the refrigerator.

Orange wine is highly aromatic and can be used to flavor a variety of desserts, such as fruit salads, brioches, etc. It will keep for several weeks in a sealed bottle.

Prepare the grapefruit sugar: scrub the grapefruit under warm, running water and pat dry. Peel off the zest in long strips, taking care that no pith is attached. Pour ⅛ cup (30 g) sugar onto a plate. Coat the strips of grapefruit zest in the sugar, arrange them on a baking sheet and place them in the oven on its very lowest setting for 3 hours to dry them out. Transfer to a blender and grind to a powder.

Prepare the fresh basil sorbet: pour 2 cups (50 cl) water into a saucepan, and add 1 generous cup (210 g) sugar and ½ cup (55 g) glucose. Dissolve the sugar over a low heat, then bring to a boil. Add the sprig of basil, then remove from the heat and leave to infuse until the syrup is completely cold.

Squeeze the juice from the lemon pulp and strain it through a chinois (or fine sieve). Measure the juice and mix it with an equal quantity of basil syrup. Transfer the mixture to an ice-cream maker and place in the freezer. Shred 4 basil leaves and add them when the blades stop turning.

Orange wine
- **2 oranges**
- **½ lemon**
- **¾ cup (2 dl) neutral flavored fruit spirit**
- **1 cup (200 g) sugar**
- **1 quart (1 l) rosé wine**
- **Few drops vanilla essence or 1 vanilla pod**

Special utensils
- **Ice-cream maker**
- **4 cake pans, 2 inches (6 cm) in diameter**
- **1 cookie cutter, 4 inches (10 cm) in diameter**

● **Choose good Menton lemons with their green leaves.**

● **Cut both ends off each lemon.**

● **Cut around the inside of the lemons to extract the cylinder of pulp.**

● **Plunge the shells, cut-off ends and lemon leaves in 2 cups (50 cl) water with ½ cup (100 g) sugar.**

● Scrub the lemon under warm, running water, pat dry, then grate the zest on a fine grater.

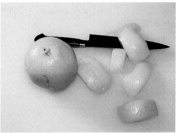

● Peel off the grapefruit zest with a knife, taking care that no pith is attached.

● Roll the strips of zest in ⅛ cup (30 g) sugar so that they are thoroughly coated.

● Arrange the grapefruit zests on a baking sheet and leave them to dry in the oven.

Pour ½ cup (10 cl) of basil syrup into a saucepan and reduce to a syrupy consistency. Shred the remaining 4 basil leaves. Add the shredded basil to the syrup, remove from the heat and leave to infuse and cool.

Prepare the glazed tartlets: preheat the oven to 325°F (160°; gas mark 3). Butter 4 cake pans, 2 inches (6 cm) in diameter. Roll 4 ounces (100 g) of dough on a lightly floured work surface. Cut 4 rounds, 4 inches (10 cm) in diameter and place them in the buttered pans. Prick the bases with a fork.

Mix the grapefruit sugar with 1 tablespoon flour. Spoon the mixture into the tartlets. Add 1 tablespoon (10 g) butter, cut into small dice, to each tartlet. Bake the tartlets in the oven for 8-10 minutes. After they have been cooking for 4 minutes, add 1 tablespoon orange wine to each tartlet and return to the oven. At this point, the orange wine and grapefruit sugar will have formed a thick, treacly syrup. Remove the tartlets from the pans and place on a rack.

● Bring 1 generous cup (210 g) sugar to a boil with 2 cups (50 cl) water and a ½ cup (55 g) glucose. Add the basil.

● Measure the juice and mix it with an equal quantity of basil syrup.

● Roll out the dough on a lightly floured work surface.

● Cut out 4 rounds of dough, 4 inches (10 cm) in diameter.

The tartlets can be gently reheated in a very low oven for 3-4 minutes. Place a warm tartlet on each plate. Fill the lemon shells with basil-flavored lemon sorbet and arrange alongside the tartlets. Place the lemon "lids" with the lemon leaves on top. Surround with a little of the basil infusion.

Frédéric Robert, pastry chef at the Louis XV *in Monaco and the* Restaurant Alain Ducasse *in Paris is a loyal friend and colleague of the master chef. Some years ago, Alain Ducasse asked him to perfect the recipe for candied Menton lemons. He could not have paid a more fitting tribute to the Menton region or to the quality of this citrus fruit synonymous with the Mediterranean.*

Wine suggestion: Corsican Muscat, D. Gentile, 1990.

● Place the rounds of dough in the buttered pans.

● Sprinkle grapefruit sugar into the tartlets, adding 1 tablespoon (10 g) diced butter to each one.

● After they have been cooking for 4 minutes, add 1 tablespoon orange wine to each tartlet.

● Using an icing bag, fill the candied lemon shells with lemon sorbet.

" FOR ALAIN DUCASSE, THE LEMON AND ALL CITRUS FRUITS ARE THE OTHER "SIGNATURE" OF THE MEDITER-RANEAN. HE PARTICULARLY CHERISHES THE LEMON TREE, WHOSE BLOSSOM SCENTS THE AIR ALL YEAR ROUND AND, AS YOU BRUSH PAST THE LEAVES, THEY, TOO, GIVE OFF A SUBTLE PERFUME. "

CONTENTS

● Alain Ducasse ●
Candied Menton Lemons, Filled with Fresh Basil Sorbet and Glazed Grapefruit Tartlets

In this dessert, Alain Ducasse draws on virtually the entire spectrum of citrus fruits, using each of them in one or more different ways to exploit their virtues, highlighted by the fresh flavor of basil. The grapefruit zest lends subtle bitterness and the lemon sorbet a touch of acidity to the aromatic candied lemons. Orange wine is a very ancient Provençal tradition and its distinctive bitter notes add an elegant finishing touch to the dish.

● Franck Cerutti ●
Menton Lemon Tartlets

A glowing tribute to the lemon, featured in this recipe in every possible guise (flesh, juice and zest). It is absolutely imperative to choose lemons of the very finest quality for this dessert. The flesh, used plain and simple, should be very sweet and not at all acid. What a pleasure it is to bite into the juicy segments, to feel the delicately acidulated custard coating the palate and to crunch the dried lemon slices.

•Jean-Louis Nomicos•
Scallops with Citrus Fruits and Salsify

Jean-Louis Nomicos uses candied citrus fruit zest to add a surprising touch of sweetness to savory dishes. This recipe centers around a bitter-sweet interplay of flavors between Belgian endive, caramelized salsify and citrus zests. The orange segments and a dash of lemon juice lend a sunny note to this winter dish. The diverse textures of the garnish, (crunchy endives, smooth salsify and juicy orange) counterbalance the melt-in-the-mouth scallops.

•Sylvain Portay•
Floating Citrus Islands

This is a variation on "floating islands". The "islands" in this case resemble lemon tartlets, but the crust is replaced by the meringues traditionally associated with the classic dessert. Practically all the commonest citrus fruits are used : the meringue is flavored with lime zest, lemon adds a hint of acidity to the custard, while the flesh and juice of grapefruit and two types of orange provide freshness.

•Jean-François Piège•
Duck with a Citrus Glaze and Giblet Melba

This is a new interpretation of the classic theme of duck *à l'orange*, taking advantage of every part of the duck. The *aiguilletes* (the thin slices of meat on either side of the breastbone), together with all the giblets, are served with a rich duck sauce made from the legs. The most important feature, however, is the touch of bitterness provided by oranges in their various guises : marmalade, grated zests coating the meat and Amer Picon, enhanced by the acidity of lemon juice.

•Alessandro Stratta•
Salad of Marinated Abalone, Belgian Endive and Radicchio with Pink Grapefruit and Lemon

This refreshing salad provides a fascinating interplay between the acidity of lemon, the subtle bitterness of grapefruit and the salad vegetables, the piquancy of radishes and the fragrant taste of basil dressing. It also offers a sophisticated textural contrast between the crispness of Belgian endive, radicchio and radishes, the fleshy feel of lamb's lettuce, the freshness of grapefruit segments and the elasticity of the marinated shellfish.

Menton Lemon Tartlets

BY FRANCK CERUTTI

Prepare the dough: scrub the lemon under warm, running water, pat dry and finely grate the zest. Quickly knead together the flour, the finely diced butter, egg and lemon zest to obtain a smooth dough. Roll into a ball, encase in saran wrap and leave to rest in the refrigerator for at least 2 hours.

Prepare the lemon custard: scrub the lemons under warm, running water, pat dry and finely grate the zest. Squeeze the lemons. Place 3 eggs and 2 egg yolks in a saucepan with the grated zest, lemon juice, sugar and butter. Mix thoroughly and cook over a very low heat for 15-25 minutes, stirring constantly, but do not allow the mixture to boil. Remove from the heat as soon as the custard coats the spatula. Pour immediately into a bowl and leave to cool.

Prepare the lemons for the decoration: scrub 1 lemon under warm, running water, pat dry and cut into very thin slices. Arrange the slices on a nonstick baking sheet and dry in the oven, on its very lowest setting, for 1 ½ hours.

Peel the other 8 lemons completely, taking care to remove the pith. Divide into segments and remove the surrounding membrane. Arrange the segments on a small rack.
Pour 2 ¼ cups (500 g) sugar and 1 quart (1 l) water into a wide saucepan. Stir over a low heat to dissolve the sugar, then bring to a boil. Plunge the rack into the syrup and poach the lemon segments for 2 minutes, then remove from the water and drain.

Arrange the segments on baking parchment and bake in the oven at 200°F (100°C; gas mark ¼) for 10 minutes to glaze them.

Make the lemon and lime sauce: Squeeze the lemons and limes and strain the juice. Melt the sugar in a saucepan with 2 tablespoons water. Bring to a boil and cook to obtain a pale caramel. Remove from the heat and add the lemon and lime juice. Take care, the mixture may spit. Return the pan to the heat and reduce to a syrup. Heat the lemon marmalade gently to soften, then strain through a chinois (or fine sieve) and stir into the syrup.

Finish the tartlets: preheat the oven to 350°F (180°C; gas mark 4). Butter 8 cake pans, 4 inches (10 cm) in diameter. Lightly flour the work surface and roll out the dough to a thickness of ⅛ inch (3 mm). Cut out 8 rounds about 5 inches (12 cm) in diameter. Line the cake pans with the pastry, removing the surplus dough by running the rolling pin around the edges. Prick the bases with a fork. Bake in the oven for 15 minutes. Turn the pastry cases out of the pans immediately and leave to cool on a rack.

Fill the pastry cases with the custard and arrange the lemon segments in a rosette pattern on top. Sprinkle with confectioners' sugar and decorate with slices of dried lemon. Surround with a little lemon and lime sauce.

4 SERVINGS

DOUGH

- 1 ¾ cups (250 g) flour
- 1 ½ sticks (150 g) unsalted butter
- Generous 1/4 cup (65 g) sugar
- 1 egg
- 1 lemon

LEMON CUSTARD

- 3 lemons
- 3 eggs plus 2 egg yolks
- 1 ¼ cups (270 g) sugar
- 1 ½ sticks (150 g) unsalted butter

TO DECORATE

- 9 Menton lemons
- 2 ½ cups (500 g) sugar
- Confectioners' sugar

LEMON AND LIME SAUCE

- 5 lemons
- 5 limes
- 2 tablespoons (70 g) sugar
- 3 tablespoons (60 g) lemon
  marmalade

SPECIAL UTENSILS

- 8 cake pans, 4 inches (10 cm) in
  diameter
- 1 cookie cutter 5 inches (12 cm) in
  diameter

*Wine suggestion: Corsican Muscat,
D. Gentile, 1990.*

Scallops with Citrus Fruits and Salsify

BY JEAN-LOUIS NOMICOS

Scrub the orange and lemon under running water and pat dry. Peel 4 strips of zest from each fruit, ensuring that there is no pith attached. Place in a small saucepan of cold water, bring to a boil, drain then repeat the same process once more. Dissolve 1 tablespoon (25 g) sugar in 4 tablespoons (5 cl) water. Add the orange and lemon zests and simmer over a very low heat for 2 hours. Squeeze the orange and lemon.

When the strips of zest are cold, cut them diagonally into 2 ½ inch x 1 ¼ inch (6 cm x 3 cm) pieces. Arrange on baking parchment and dry in the oven at its very lowest setting for 2 hours.

Open the scallop shells and remove the flesh and beards. Wash, drain and dry the flesh and beards. Refrigerate the scallops.

Coarsely chop the beards. Take a strip of zest from the orange and another from the lemon. Soften the scallop beards in 1 tablespoon olive oil for 5 minutes over a low heat. Add the cardamom and the orange and lemon zests. Add a generous tablespoon orange juice and scrape the base of the pan with a spatula. Add ½ cup (10 cl) light chicken stock. Add the crushed peppercorns and cook for 20 minutes over a low heat. Strain through a chinois (or fine sieve), pressing down hard on the contents with a spatula to obtain 1 ½ cups (40 cl) of juice.

Peel the salsify and wash in water with lemon juice. Cut diagonally into 24 chunks, 2 ½ inches (6 cm) long. Drain on a cloth.

Place half the salsify in a skillet with salt, pepper, 1 tablespoon (20 g) cane sugar and 2 tablespoons (30 g) butter. Add enough chicken stock to cover. Place the rest of the salsify in another skillet with salt, pepper and 2 tablespoons (30 g) butter, with enough chicken stock to cover. Cook both lots of salsify, covered, for 30 minutes over a low heat. The first lot will be brown, the other white, but both should be glossy and tender.

Remove the outer leaves of the baby Belgian endive. Cut each leaf into 4 and cook for 2 minutes in a nonstick skillet with 1 ½ tablespoons (20 g) butter, salt, pepper and ½ tablespoon (10 g) cane sugar, until crisp.

Separate a few orange segments and remove the surrounding membrane. Melt 4 tablespoons (50 g) butter in a skillet. When the butter turns nut-brown, add 2 tablespoons lemon juice, scraping the base of the pan with a spatula. Add 2 ounces (50 g) of orange segments and the pan juices from the scallop beards. Season with salt and pepper. Sir in a few drops of balsamic vinegar and lemon juice.

Season the scallops with salt and pepper. Seal them on both sides in a nonstick skillet with 1 tablespoon olive oil. Add 2 tablespoons (30 g) butter. Cook for 1 minute more on each side, basting with butter.

Pour a little sauce onto each plate. Arrange the brown and white salsify in an alternating patter on top of the sauce. Add the scallops and season them with fine salt and black pepper. Finish with the candied orange and lemon zests.

4 SERVINGS

- 12 scallops in their shells, each weighing 13 ounces (380 g)
- 1 unwaxed orange
- 1 unwaxed lemon
- 1 tablespoon (25 g) superfine sugar
- 2 tablespoons olive oil
- 2 cardamom pods
- 1 ½ cups (40 cl) light chicken stock (see page 130)
- 6 Sarawak (Malaysian) peppercorns
- 1 ¾ pounds (800 g) salsify
- 1 ½ tablespoons (30 g) cane sugar
- 1 ½ sticks (160 g) unsalted butter
- 2 baby Belgian endives
- Balsamic vinegar
- Fine salt
- Salt, freshly ground black pepper

Wine suggestion: a full-bodied, complex white Bordeaux, such as Pessac-Léognan, Château Laville Haut-Brion, 1996.

Duck with a Citrus Glaze and Giblet Melba

BY JEAN-FRANÇOIS PIÈGE

Season the insides of the ducklings with salt and pepper. Place 6 orange flowers and 6 orange leaves inside each bird and leave to stand for 24 hours.

Prepare the bitter orange marmalade: scrub the oranges under warm, running water, pat dry and peel away the zest, taking care that there is no pith attached. Cut half the zest into rectangles ½ inch x 1 ½ inches (1 cm x 4 cm). Finely mince the rest and dry in the oven on its very lowest setting for 2 hours.

Squeeze the oranges and strain the juice through a chinois (or fine sieve). Pour the orange juice into a stainless steel saucepan and add the rectangles of orange zest, ¼ cup (50 g) sugar and the orange leaves. Simmer gently over a very low heat for 3-4 hours, without allowing the mixture to boil.

Prepare the *jus* for the duck sauce: chop the duck legs into pieces and brown in a cast iron stew pot with the duck fat. Skim off some of the fat. Add the carrots cut into diagonal chunks, the scallions cut into rings and the diced tomatoes. Cover and soften the vegetables for 5 minutes over a low heat. Heat and flambé the wine. Heat the duck *jus*. Add the Amer Picon to the pot, scraping the base with a spatula, and reduce. Add the wine, again scraping the base of the pot and reducing until no liquid remains, then add the duck *jus*, ginger, peppercorns and *bouquet garni*. Transfer to the oven at 230°F (120°C; gas mark ¼-½) and cook for 3 hours.

Prepare the giblet melba: place the heart, brains and tongues in a saucepan of cold water and bring to a boil. Boil for 2 minutes, then drain. Place the tongues in a small ovenproof skillet with enough chicken stock to cover and cook in the oven at 230°F (120°C; gas mark ¼-½) for 2 hours. When the tongues are cooked, remove the cartilage.

Place the ducklings in a cast iron stew pot, cover and place in the oven at 450°F (230°C; gas mark 8). To obtain pale pink meat, roast for 20 minutes, for medium cooked meat, roast for 25 minutes. Leave the ducks to rest for 10 minutes in a warm place.

Continue the giblet melba: quickly broil the *foie gras*, heart and *gésiers* (ducks' gizzards preserved in their own fat). Season the *foie gras* with fine salt and *mignonette* (coarsely ground white) pepper. Place the butter in a skillet. When it is nut-brown, fry the tongues, kidneys, gizzards and brains until golden. Skim off the fat. Add the lemon juice, scraping the base of the pan with a spatula.

After 3 hours, the duck sauce should be syrupy. Strain through a chinois (or fine sieve). Finely mince the liver and heart and use them to bind the sauce, stirring briskly with a balloon whisk. Add 1 tablespoon of orange marmalade. Adjust the seasoning, then add the pan juices produced by the ducks. Strain and stir in the rectangles of candied orange zest.

Mix the giblets and *foie gras* in a skillet. Add a tablespoon of duck sauce and stir carefully. Toast the bread. Spread the slices of toast with the mixture and sprinkle with celery leaves.

Just before serving, coat the duck breasts with orange marmalade. Roll in dried, minced orange zest and glaze under the grill for 2-3 minutes. Detach the breast meat and season with fine salt and pepper.

Arrange the duck breast on 2 plates with the giblet melba alongside. Spoon a little sauce onto the plates and serve the rest separately.

4 SERVINGS

- 2 best-quality "smothered" Bresse ducklings (slaughtered by smothering rather than bleeding)
- 12 orange flowers and 12 orange leaves
- Fine salt, freshly ground pepper

BITTER ORANGE MARMALADE
- 6 ½ pounds (3 kg) bitter oranges with about 10 leaves
- ¼ cup (50 g) sugar

DUCK SAUCE
- 4 tablespoons (50 g) duck fat
- 4 ounces (100 g) each, carrot, scallions, tomatoes
- 2 cups (50 cl) red wine
- 1 quart (1 l) duck jus (adapted from the recipe for squab jus, page 104)
- 2 tablespoons Amer Picon (orange-based aperitif or digestif)
- ¾ ounce (20 g) fresh ginger root, sliced
- 10 black peppercorns
- 1 bouquet garni
- Orange marmalade

GIBLET MELBA
- 1 heart, 2 brains, 2 tongues, 2 gizzards taken from 2 fat ducks
- 1 ¼ cups (30 cl) chicken stock
- 4 ounces (100 g) foie gras in two slices
- 2 gésiers (ducks' gizzards preserved in their own fat)
- 2 duck's kidneys
- ½ stick butter, juice of 1 lemon
- 2 slices farmhouse bread
- 2 ounces (50 g) celery leaf sprigs
- Mignonette (coarsely ground white) pepper

Wine suggestion: a white wine from the Rhône Valley, such as Châteauneuf-du-Pape, Château Rayas, L. Reynaud, 1995.

Floating Citrus Islands

BY SYLVAIN PORTAY

Prepare the meringue: preheat the oven to 425°F (220°C; gas mark 7). Squeeze the lemon half. Grate the zest of the lime half. Place the egg whites, lemon juice and lime zest in a blender. Process the whites until they peak, adding one-third of the sugar at a time.

Place 4 round cookie cutters, 3 inches (8 cm) in diameter and 2 inches (5 cm) deep on a nonstick baking sheet. Transfer the meringue to an icing bag and fill the cutters with meringue. Cook in the oven for 4 minutes. As soon as they have finished cooking, place the baking sheet in a cool place and leave the meringues to rest for at least 1 hour, without removing the cutters.

Prepare the lemon custard: break the whole eggs into a bowl, add the 2 egg yolks and whisk with the sugar until the mixture turns white. Pour the lemon juice into a saucepan and bring to a boil. Whisk the egg and sugar mixture into the pan. Boil for 2-3 minutes, whisking constantly. Remove from the heat and stir in the diced butter.

Prepare the sauce: squeeze the orange, the blood orange and the grapefruit. Strain the citrus juices into a saucepan and warm gently. Add the sugar and pectin (optional). Bring the mixture to a boil, whisking constantly. Remove from the heat and leave to cool.

Prepare the decoration: peel the orange, blood orange and grapefruit with a small, very sharp knife, making sure to remove the pith. Separate the segments and remove all the membranes.

Finish the floating islands. Gently remove the cookie cutters and carefully hollow out the meringues, leaving a 1-inch (1.5 cm) border. Arrange the meringues in the center of 4 heat-resistant soup plates. Transfer the custard to an icing bag and fill the meringues. Slide the plates under the grill and caramelize for 1-2 minutes. Decorate with orange and grapefruit segments and surround with sauce. Serve immediately.

4 SERVINGS

MERINGUE

- 4 or 5 egg whites
  (½ cup or 200 g)
- ½ lemon
- ½ lime
- ¾ cup (130 g) sugar

LEMON CUSTARD

- 5 eggs plus 2 egg yolks
- ½ cup (90 g) sugar
- 1 cup (25 cl) lemon juice
- Scant ½ cup (90 g) unsalted butter

SAUCE

- 1 orange
- 1 blood orange
- 1 pink grapefruit
- ⅛ cup (30 g) sugar
- 1 teaspoon (5 g) pectin (optional)

TO DECORATE

- 1 orange
- 1 blood orange
- 1 pink grapefruit

SPECIAL UTENSILS

- 4 round cookie cutters, 3 inches
  (8 cm) in diameter and 2 inches
  (5 cm) deep, to use as templates

Wine suggestion: a white wine from south-western France, such as Jurançon "Quintessence du Petit Manseng", Domaine Cauhapé, Henri Ramonteu, 1989.

Salad of Marinated Abalone, Belgian Endive and Radicchio with Pink Grapefruit and Lemon

BY ALESSANDRO STRATTA

Using an electric carving knife, cut the abalone or ormers into paper-thin slices and then into fine julienne. Place them in a salad bowl. Halve and squeeze the lemon. Drizzle the contents of the bowl with 1 tablespoon lemon juice, salt and pepper. Add 3 tablespoons olive oil. Leave to marinate for 3-4 hours in the refrigerator.

Prepare the accompaniment: preheat the oven to 275°F (140°C; gas mark 1). Peel and wash the potato and cut it onto a long, thick oval. Cut it on a mandolin, turning to each time so that each slice looks like a waffle. Heat the clarified butter. Coat the potato waffles in the hot butter, then arrange them side by side on a nonstick baking sheet and sprinkle with coarse salt. Cook in the oven for 20-25 minutes until crisp and golden. Reserve at room temperature.

Rinse the radishes. Cut the red radish in fine julienne. Peel the white radish and slice very thinly on a mandolin. Mix the two radishes in a bowl with the celery leaves and chervil.

Peel the grapefruits with a small, very sharp knife, taking care to remove the pith. Separate the segments and remove the membranes and pits. Add the grapefruit segments to the radishes.

Mix 1 generous tablespoon lemon juice with salt, pepper and 4 tablespoons olive oil and mix to create an emulsion. Toss the radishes and grapefruit in the lemon dressing.

Wash the lamb's lettuce and pat dry. Wash and thinly slice the Belgian endive. Wash the radicchio heart and cut into strips. Carefully mix the three salad ingredients with the abalone and minced chives.

Rinse the basil, pat dry, tear off the leaves and place them in a blender. Add ½ cup (10 cl) olive oil in a steady stream while the blender is in motion, to obtain a smooth sauce. Season with salt.

Divide the abalone salad between 4 plates and top with the radish and grapefruit salad. Drizzle green basil sauce around the edge. Serve the potato waffle separately.

4 SERVINGS

- 8 fresh abalone or ormers
- 1 Menton lemon
- Generous ¾ cup (20 cl) olive oil
- 1 large red radish
- 1 white radish
- 2 tablespoons yellow celery leaf sprigs
- 2 tablespoons chervil leaves
- 2 pink grapefruits
- 4 ounces (100 g) lamb's lettuce
- 1 Belgian endive
- 1 radicchio heart
- 2 teaspoons
- ½ bunch basil
- Salt, freshly ground pepper

ACCOMPANIMENT

- 1 large potato
- 1 tablespoon clarified butter (see page 171)
- Coarse sea salt

Wine suggestion: a white Bordeaux, such as Graves, Clos Floridene, D. Dubourdieu.

LIST OF RECIPES

ACKNOWLEDGMENTS

ALAIN DUCASSE would especially like to thank:
Didier Elena for keeping the project on track
and for coordinating the work of his students in the true spirit of l'Atelier.
He also wishes to thank *Hervé Amiard* for slipping so unobtrusively into the kitchen
and "stealing" images of this life "not quite like any other".

● HERVÉ AMIARD would like to thank Alain Ducasse for allowing him unrestricted free access to his establishments in Paris, Monaco and Moustière-Sainte-Marie, enabling him to see "behind the scenes". He also wishes to thank Didier Elena.

ALAIN DUCASSE and HERVÉ AMIARD would like to thank the following for their help in the creation of the book and photographs, and especially for their kindness and warm welcome: Monsieur Bonaldo at Alma di Taggia, Italy; the Blanc family at Villelaure; Monsieur Lecoq at Précy-sur-Marne; Monsieur Rossano at Vezza di Alba, Italy: Max and his family for the sea bass fishing; Monsieur Gallen and the Ménestral team at Audierne; Alessandro Stratta, Sylvain Portay, Jean-Louis Nomicos, Jean-François Nomicos and all the brigade at the Restaurant Alain Ducasse in Paris, and Franck Cerutti and all the restaurant team at Le Louis XV-Alain Ducasse in Monaco.

All Hervé Amiard's photographs were taken with Kodak professional ektachrome E 100 S and Kodak T-MAX, and Nikon photographic equipment. The Kodak films were developed by the Rush-Labo laboratory, Paris. Hervé Amiard is grateful to these companies for their trust, and especially wishes to thank M. Denis Cuisy and M. Guy Bourreau.

●

ADDRESSES

● ALAIN DUCASSE
Restaurant Alain Ducasse
59, avenue Raymond-Poincaré - 75016 Paris
Tel: +33 1 47 27 12 27
http : //www.alain-ducasse.com

WHERE TO FIND ALAIN DUCASSE'S STUDENTS:

● FRANCK CERUTTI
Le Louis XV
Hôtel de Paris - Place du Casino
Monte-Carlo - 98000 Monaco
Tel: +377 92 16 30 01

● JEAN-LOUIS NOMICOS
Pavillon de la Grande Cascade
Allée de Longchamp - Bois de Boulogne
75016 Paris
Tel: +33 1 45 27 33 51

● JEAN-FRANÇOIS PIÈGE
Restaurant Alain Ducasse
59, avenue Raymond-Poincaré - 75016 Paris
Tel: +33 1 47 27 12 27

● SYLVAIN PORTAY
Ritz Carlton Hotel
600 Stockton at California Street
San Francisco, California - USA
Tel: 415 296 7465

● ALESSANDRO STRATTA
Renoir
The Mirage Hotel & Casino
3400 Las Vegas Blvd South
Las Vegas, Nevada - USA
Tel: 702 791 7223